SIMPLY

PHILOSOPHY

DK LONDON

Project Editor Rose Blackett-Ord
US Editor Kayla Dugger
Senior Art Editor Phil Gamble
Editors Andrew Szudek, Kathryn Hill
Assistant Editor Daniel Byrne
Senior Designer Mark Cavanagh
Managing Editor Gareth Jones
Senior Managing Art Editor Lee Griffiths
Senior Production Editor Andy Hilliard
Senior Production Controller Rachel Ng
Jacket Design Development Manager
Sophia M.T.T.
Jacket Designer Akiko Kato
Associate Publishing Director Liz Wheeler
Art Director Karen Self
Publishing Director Jonathan Metcalf

First American Edition, 2021
Published in the United States by DK Publishing
1450 Broadway, Suite 801, New York, NY 10018

Copyright © 2021 Dorling Kindersley Limited
DK, a Division of Penguin Random House LLC
22 23 24 25 10 9 8 7 6 5 4 3 2
004–319157–Feb/2021

A catalog record for this book
is available from the Library of Congress.
ISBN 978-0-7440-2739-6

Printed and bound in China

For the curious
www.dk.com

FSC
www.fsc.org
MIX
Paper from
responsible sources
FSC™ C018179

CONSULTANT

Marcus Weeks studied music and
philosophy in college and worked as
a teacher, piano restorer, and musician
before embarking on a career as a writer.
He has authored and contributed to
numerous books on philosophy,
psychology, and the arts.

CONTRIBUTORS

Douglas Burnham is an emeritus
professor of philosophy at Staffordshire
University. He has written extensively
on Kant, Nietzsche, and aesthetics.

Daniel Byrne is an editor and writer who
studied philosophy at Oxford Brookes
University. He has a particular interest
in social and political philosophy.

Robert Fletcher holds degrees in
philosophy from Reading, Nottingham,
and Oxford Universities. He is a retired
teacher and academic but still works
as a tutor for the University of Oxford's
Department for Continuing Education.

Andrew Szudek is a writer and editor
who studied philosophy at Cambridge
University, specializing in Wittgenstein
and the philosophy of mind.

Marianne Talbot is the director of
studies in philosophy at the Department
for Continuing Education, University of
Oxford. She has worked for the colleges
of Oxford University since 1987.

David Webb is a professor of philosophy
at Staffordshire University. His interests
include science; historical epistemology;
politics; and the work of Bachelard,
Foucault, and Serres.

CONTENTS

BEING AND LANGUAGE

MIND AND MATTER

RIGHT AND WRONG

POLITICS AND POWER

LOGIC AND ARGUMENT

WHAT IS PHILOSOPHY?

"Philosophy," Plato said, "begins in wonder." It was from our natural curiosity about the world and our place within it that philosophy emerged. In the ancient world, people wondered about the things they saw and experienced and questioned why the world is the way it is. Religion of one sort or another provided some answers, describing natural events as the actions of gods or spirits, but in the early civilizations, people wanted explanations that satisfied their capacity for rational thought.

The foundations of Western philosophy, which focused on reason and observation, were laid by Greek scholars in the 6th century BCE. Thinkers such as Thales and Democritus studied the physical world— its structure and what it is made of—and their theories paved the way for the development of the physical sciences many centuries later. At roughly the same time, thinkers in India and China pondered similar questions from different cultural and religious perspectives. As their societies became more sophisticated, the early philosophers in both the East and the West turned their attention to the human world. They asked questions about the nature of suffering, how we should live our lives, and how it is that we can understand the world at all.

Throughout history, there have been many different schools of philosophical thought, and their ideas have often directly opposed each other. But philosophy is about asking questions, examining ideas, and taking part in debate and rational argument. Rather than providing definitive answers, philosophy is, above all, an active process of considering the fundamental questions about the universe and our place in it. It is not just the domain of academic philosophers; it is an activity we can all take part in—and we already do, when we look at the universe we live in and wonder.

THIN
ABOU
WORL

KING
THE
D

Philosophy began as an attempt to understand the world without relying on religious or mythological ideas. It was centred around two general questions: "What is the nature of reality?" (the subject of metaphysics) and "What is the nature of knowledge?" (the subject of epistemology). Answers to these questions fell into two main schools of thought: rationalism, which treated reasoning as the most reliable source of knowledge, and empiricism, which stressed the importance of sensory experience. Early philosophers were the scientists of their day; the physical sciences only became distinct from philosophy in the 17th century.

Myth
Before the Milesians,
the Greeks believed that
natural events, such as storms,
were caused by the gods.

Nature
The Milesians argued that
myths about gods were often
irrational and were not needed
to explain natural events.

ABANDONING MYTH

The first Western philosophers lived in the Greek city-state of Miletus in the 6th century BCE. The Milesian school, as it was called, questioned the belief that gods exist, claiming instead that there is a natural order to the world. Relying on reason and observation alone, the Milesians set out to find the *arche* (underlying principle) of the cosmos. Their studies paved the way for future scientific and philosophical thought.

"Intellect is the swiftest of things, for it runs through everything."
Thales of Miletus

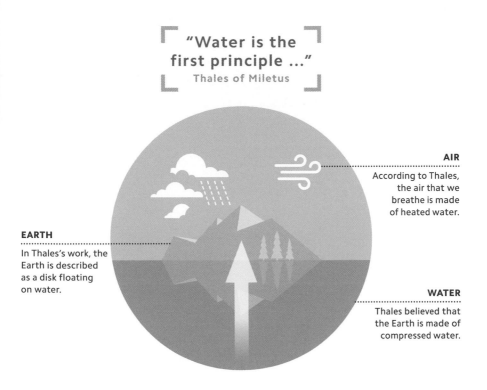

> "Water is the first principle ..."
> Thales of Miletus

AIR

According to Thales, the air that we breathe is made of heated water.

EARTH

In Thales's work, the Earth is described as a disk floating on water.

WATER

Thales believed that the Earth is made of compressed water.

A SINGLE SOURCE

Over many years, Thales of Miletus (c.624–c.546 BCE) observed that an island in a local river was increasing in size. He knew that water was versatile—that it froze when cooled and became steam when heated—so he proposed that water was condensing into earth and enlarging the island. From these and other observations, he concluded that water is the source of all things. His fellow philosopher Anaximenes (c.585–c.525 BCE) disagreed: he claimed that air, not water, is the primary substance.

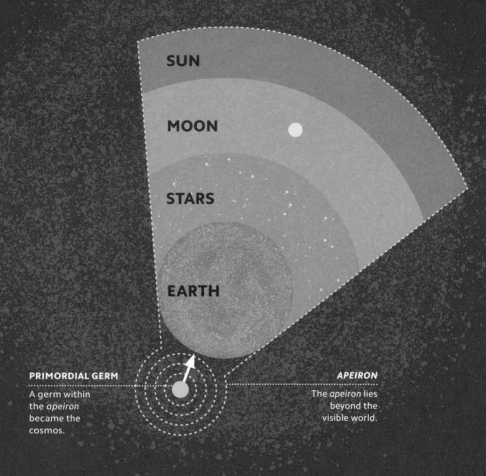

SUN

MOON

STARS

EARTH

PRIMORDIAL GERM
A germ within
the *apeiron*
became the
cosmos.

APEIRON
The *apeiron* lies
beyond the
visible world.

AN UNKNOWABLE ORIGIN

Anaximander (c.610–546 BCE) questioned how water or
air could be primary substances (see p.11). He claimed the
world was once a germ that was born from an unknowable
substance called the "*apeiron*" ("the indefinite"). In the
beginning, opposing forces—such as hot and cold, and dry
and wet—emerged from the germ, creating the Earth,
with the stars, the Moon, and the Sun around it.

NUMBERS RULE

Pythagoras (c.570–c.495 BCE) argued that the world is governed by numbers. For example, he discovered that the same musical note is repeated at a higher pitch when the string it is played on is halved in length. He similarly found mathematical relationships between these and other notes, forming a scale of eight notes (an octave). His followers took this idea further and claimed that the distances between the Sun, the Moon, and the planets correspond to the intervals between musical notes, creating a kind of music: the "harmony of the spheres."

HIGH A

G

F

E

D

C

B

LOW A

The octave
Pythagoras discovered that if a musical string sounds the note A, a string half its length will play the same note an octave higher.

"Number is the ruler of forms and ideas."
Pythagoras

EVERYTHING FLOWS

WATER
When cooled, vapor becomes water, which forms lakes.

Heraclitus (c.535–c.475 BCE) claimed that the underlying basis of everything is change. He argued that the cosmos is a battleground of opposing forces, but that rather than being harmful, this conflict sustains the world. Just as light requires dark, day requires night and life requires death. He called the principle that governs change the "logos."

VAPOR
When heated, water becomes vapor, which forms clouds.

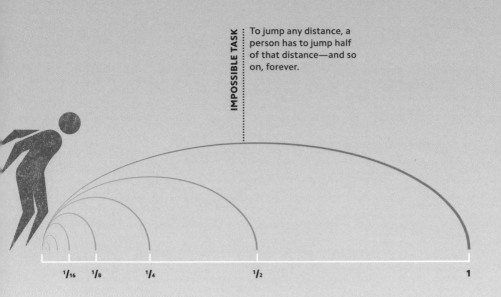

IMPOSSIBLE TASK

To jump any distance, a person has to jump half of that distance—and so on, forever.

¹/₁₆ ¹/₈   ¹/₄   ¹/₂   1

CHANGE IS IMPOSSIBLE

Zeno of Elea (c.490–430 BCE) claimed that change (see opposite) is impossible and that any changes that people see are illusions. For example, in an argument known as a paradox (which shows that something unlikely must be true), he showed that for someone to move any distance, they have to travel half of that distance first. However, in order to do that, they would first have to travel half of *that* distance, and so on, indefinitely. Because a distance can always be halved, any movement requires traveling an infinite number of half-distances, which is impossible. From this, Zeno was able to conclude that movement is an illusion.

Original ship
To begin with, the ship is in perfect condition.

Parts replaced
As the years pass, damaged parts of the ship are replaced.

THE SHIP OF THESEUS

A thought experiment from Ancient Greece concerns the nature of identity. If the component parts of an object are replaced over time, does it remain the same object? To illustrate the problem, the Greeks used the example of the legendary ship of Theseus, which was completely restored over the course of a century.

Additional repairs
More and more parts of the ship are restored.

Restored ship
Finally, every part has been replaced—but is it the same ship?

ETERNAL ATOMS

Leucippus (early 5th century BCE) and Democritus (c.460–371 BCE) argued that matter could not be divided infinitely, and so had to be composed of indivisible building blocks—which they called "atoms." They thought that atoms must exist in a void, which enables them to move around and combine with other atoms to form different substances. They also believed that atoms are eternal and unchanging: when an object disintegrates, its atoms survive and recombine to form new substances. This means that the atoms that make up the human body are not destroyed after death, but are dispersed to become something else.

Round atoms
According to Democritus, atoms come in various shapes, each of which has a different property. For example, the atoms of liquids are round and smooth and move past each other easily.

THE VOID

A REALM OF IDEAS

Plato (427–347 BCE) believed that people gain knowledge
by using reason rather than relying on their senses alone (see
p.34). He noticed, for example, that we experience different
kinds of dog, but not what they have in common—that is,
the definitive, or ideal, dog. He argued that the ideal dog
exists, but in the perfect realm of Forms—a world that
we cannot see but that contains the ideal Forms of all things.
Plato claimed that reason tells us that this world must exist.

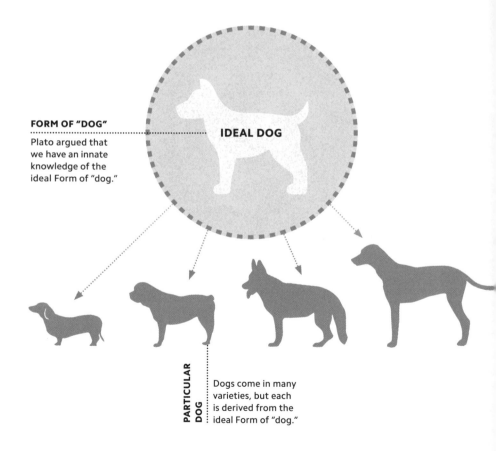

FORM OF "DOG"

Plato argued that
we have an innate
knowledge of the
ideal Form of "dog."

IDEAL DOG

PARTICULAR DOG

Dogs come in many
varieties, but each
is derived from the
ideal Form of "dog."

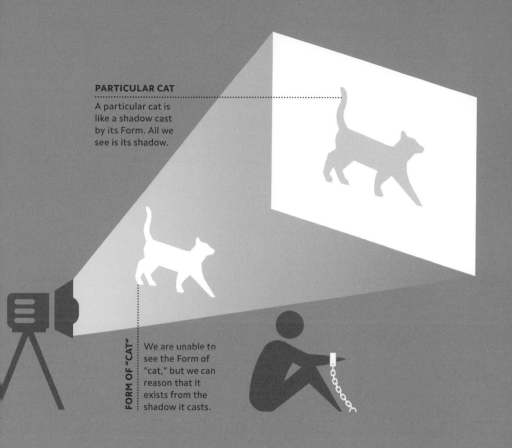

PARTICULAR CAT
A particular cat is like a shadow cast by its Form. All we see is its shadow.

FORM OF "CAT"
We are unable to see the Form of "cat," but we can reason that it exists from the shadow it casts.

A SHADOW WORLD

Plato illustrated his theory of Forms (see opposite) with an allegory. He compared human beings to prisoners in a cave who can only face in one direction: toward a wall on which shadows are moving. Behind them, objects pass in front of a light source to create the shadows that they see. For Plato, this is how poorly we perceive reality: all we see are shadows cast by the Forms. However, he claimed that we can always leave the cave—that is, perceive reality as it really is—by using reason to understand the Forms.

EARTHLY FORMS

Aristotle (384–322 BCE) rejected Plato's theory of Forms (see p.18). He argued that we only gain knowledge through experience and that the essence of a dog, for example, is the set of characteristics that dogs have in common. According to Aristotle, what makes a dog different from a giraffe is its design, and different things are designed for different purposes (see p.22). He believed that the form of a thing is like its design blueprint: it is that which turns matter (which he thought was made of four earthly elements) into a particular kind of thing.

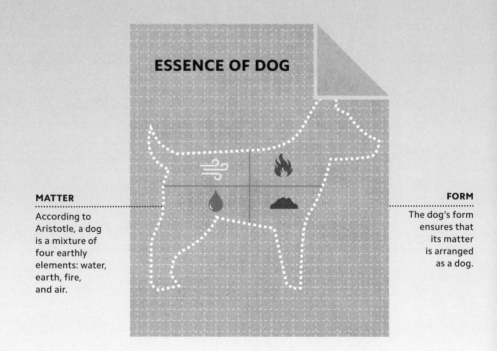

ESSENCE OF DOG

MATTER

According to Aristotle, a dog is a mixture of four earthly elements: water, earth, fire, and air.

FORM

The dog's form ensures that its matter is arranged as a dog.

Material cause
The material cause of a thing
is the matter it is made from.
In the case of a wooden chair,
its material cause is wood.

INSTRUCTIONS

Formal cause
The formal cause of a thing is its
physical design. A wooden chair's
formal cause is the blueprint
prepared by a carpenter.

Efficient cause
The efficient cause of a thing is the
process that brings it into being.
In the case of a chair, it is the work
performed by a carpenter.

Final cause
The final cause of a thing is the
purpose for which it is made.
The purpose of a chair
is to be sat on.

THE NATURE OF THINGS

For Aristotle, to know a thing is to know four things about
it: its physical makeup, its design, the circumstances that
brought it into being, and its purpose. He called these
four things "causes": the material, formal, efficient,
and final causes respectively.

Human
The purpose of a
human is to reason.
Using reason, humans
can understand the
teloi, or purposes,
of things.

EVERYTHING HAS A PURPOSE

Aristotle argued that everything has a *telos*, or purpose. The purpose of a seed, for example, is to germinate and grow into a plant, while the purpose of the plant is to bear seeds and reproduce. Likewise, the purpose of rain is to water the earth, enabling plants to grow, which in turn provide food for animals and humans.

Apple
The purpose of an
apple is to be eaten
and shed its seeds.
Its seeds then grow
into apple trees.

Clay
The purpose of clay
is to be shaped by
humans. Clay can be
shaped into bowls,
bricks, or statues.

FIRST CAUSE

If every motion has a cause, what caused the first motion? Aristotle named this the "unmoved mover."

Aristotle argued that the universe had no beginning, but that something must have set the heavenly bodies in motion. However, because everything has a cause, it follows that whatever set the heavens in motion must also have a cause. To avoid an ever-receding chain of causes, Aristotle proposed his idea of a first cause, or "unmoved mover," which set the universe in motion. Today, we could also ask: if the universe began with the Big Bang, then what caused the Big Bang?

THE UNMOVED MOVER

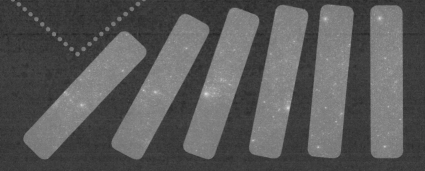

DIVINE CAUSES

Al-Ghazali (c.1058–1111) disagreed with Aristotle's idea that the heavenly bodies were set in motion at a particular time in the past (see p.23). He argued that this left no room for the will of God, which he believed was active in the world at all times. Al-Ghazali claimed that there is no necessary connection between events—that, for example, if something is placed on a fire, it does not have to burn, but it does so because God wills it. Centuries later, David Hume made a similar observation about cause and effect (see p.40).

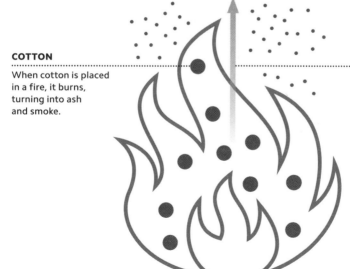

COTTON

When cotton is placed in a fire, it burns, turning into ash and smoke.

WILL OF GOD

Al-Ghazali argued that cotton does not have to burn, but it does so because God wills it to.

Under normal circumstances, our bodies seem real. However, their existence can easily be doubted.

A CERTAIN MIND

Deprived of all sensory stimulation, a person may doubt that their body exists—but not that they exist as a conscious mind or soul.

THE FLOATING MAN

Ibn Sina (c.980–1037), also known as Avicenna, imagined what it would be like for someone to float in the air with their eyes closed, receiving no information at all from their senses. In such a state, a person might imagine that their body does not exist or that their limbs are not attached to their body—but they could not doubt their existence as a conscious, thinking being. For Ibn Sina, this showed that the mind, or soul, is separate from the body—a conclusion that René Descartes drew from a similar experiment centuries later (see p.32).

DOES GOD EXIST?

St. Anselm of Canterbury (c.1033–1109) believed that the existence of God could be proved logically. He did so in six steps, in what is known as the "ontological argument" (see below).

"God has made nothing more valuable than rational existence capable of enjoying him."
St. Anselm

4
Things that exist in reality are better than things that exist in our minds.

3
Things can exist in our minds or in reality.

2
God exists as an idea in the mind.

1
God is the greatest thing that we can think of.

PHILOSOPHY

6

Therefore, God
must exist
in reality.

5

If God only existed
in our minds, he
would not be the
greatest thing
that we can
think of.

ARE RELIGION AND PHILOSOPHY COMPATIBLE?

Ibn Rushd (1126–1198), also known as Averroes, believed that religion and philosophy are compatible. He saw them as two different methods of finding the truth and argued that, because "truth cannot contradict truth," religious scholars should reinterpret scripture whenever it contradicts philosophy. Ibn Rushd distinguished between allegory (writing that has a hidden, symbolic meaning) and deduction (see p.144) and thought that when scripture defies reason, it should be interpreted allegorically.

ALLEGORY

RELIGION

GENERAL IDEAS

Universals are general ideas, such as "cat" or "triangle." Plato observed that we only ever see particular cats or triangles but never the definitive cat or triangle (see p.18). However, if people never experience general ideas, then how do we come to know them, and in what sense do they exist? These questions have given rise to two schools of philosophical thought: realism, which claims that universals exist independently of our experience, and nominalism, which claims that they are generalizations based on our experience of particular things.

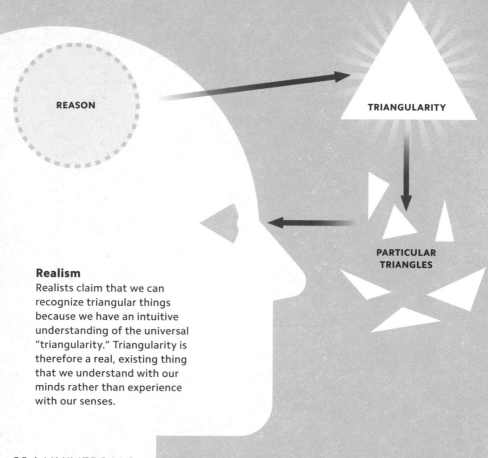

REASON

TRIANGULARITY

PARTICULAR TRIANGLES

Realism
Realists claim that we can recognize triangular things because we have an intuitive understanding of the universal "triangularity." Triangularity is therefore a real, existing thing that we understand with our minds rather than experience with our senses.

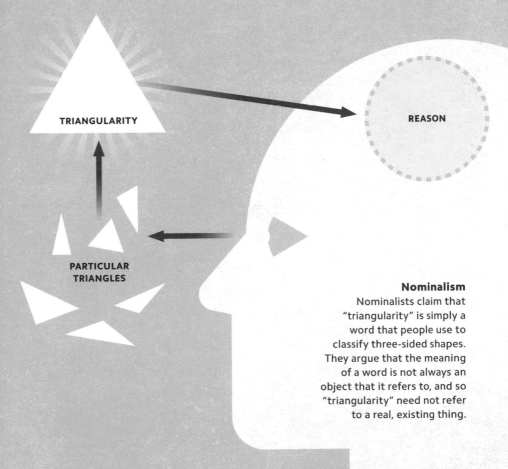

"There is no universal
outside the mind
really existing in
individual substances."
William of Ockham

TRIANGULARITY

REASON

PARTICULAR
TRIANGLES

Nominalism
Nominalists claim that
"triangularity" is simply a
word that people use to
classify three-sided shapes.
They argue that the meaning
of a word is not always an
object that it refers to, and so
"triangularity" need not refer
to a real, existing thing.

NATURE

THE MIND

THE CLOCKWORK WORLD

In the 17th century, scientists believed that the world is like a machine. Thomas Hobbes (1588–1679) agreed with this view, arguing that the universe is made purely of physical matter and that free will is an illusion. He claimed that everything runs like clockwork and that natural laws propel the world in a predetermined manner. Even our thoughts, he argued, are nothing but physical events in our brains. This idea that the universe is made of only one kind of thing is known as monism, and the idea that that thing is physical matter is known as materialism.

THE BODY

A UNIVERSE OF MINDS

Like Thomas Hobbes, Gottfried Leibniz (1646–1716) was a monist (see opposite). However, he believed that the universe is composed of mindlike entities, which he called "monads." He argued that because physical things can be divided, they cannot form the building blocks of the universe, which therefore must be nonphysical. Being nonphysical, monads do not exist in physical space, which means that they cannot interact with each other. Leibniz described them as solitary, immaterial, and infinite in number.

"Every substance is as a world apart, independent of everything else except God."
Gottfried Leibniz

I THINK, THEREFORE I AM

René Descartes (1596–1650) was a scientist who tried to answer the question, "What can I know for certain?" He applied what is known as "the method of doubt" to his beliefs, only accepting them as true if there was no other logical possibility. This process led him to believe that he could doubt absolutely everything except the fact that he was thinking and, therefore, that he existed.

Dream
Because we often feel awake in our dreams, it is possible that our experience of the world now is also a dream.

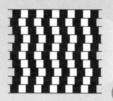

Optical illusion
We are easily deceived by optical illusions, so our senses cannot be trusted.

I THINK, THEREFORE I AM

Certainty
Everything could be an illusion except the fact that we are thinking.

Descartes' demon
Our entire life could be a hoax staged by an evil trickster.

MATTER

René Descartes doubted the existence of his body but not his existence as a thinking being (see opposite). If his body could be an illusion, however, then where were his thoughts located? His answer was that there are two worlds: the material world of the body and the immaterial world of the mind. In the material world, objects have location, mass, and shape, and everything runs like clockwork.

REALITY IS SPLIT IN TWO

MIND

In the immaterial world, our thoughts are entirely free. Descartes thought that of all creation, only humans enjoy this freedom, and that with it we can philosophize and live a spiritual life. He suggested that the material and immaterial worlds meet in the pineal gland of the brain, although he could not explain how they interact—an important topic in the field known as philosophy of mind (see pp.76–91).

TRUTHS OF REASON

Rationalism is the belief that humans gain knowledge mainly through reasoning rather than experience. It is based on the idea that our senses are unreliable, but that there are various kinds of statement (for example, "2 + 2 = 4") that cannot be doubted and that we know to be true intuitively. Many rationalists argue that all of mathematics is true in this intuitive sense, and that because reason provides us with mathematics, it may also provide us with scientific and ethical principles.

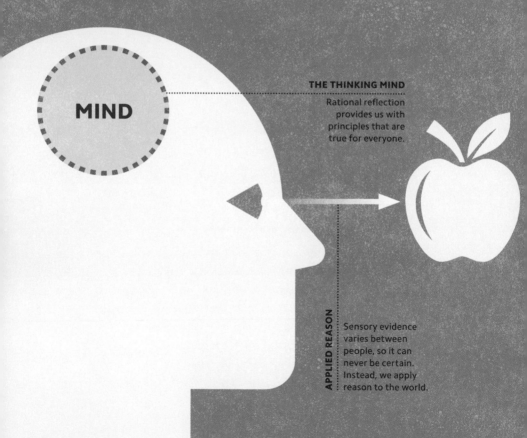

MIND

THE THINKING MIND

Rational reflection provides us with principles that are true for everyone.

APPLIED REASON

Sensory evidence varies between people, so it can never be certain. Instead, we apply reason to the world.

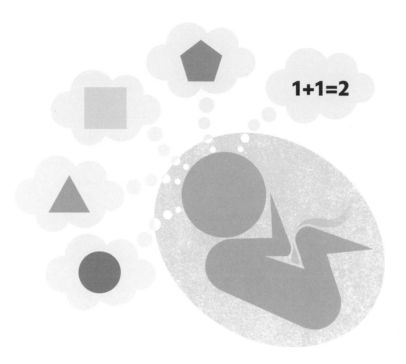

PEOPLE ARE BORN WITH IDEAS

Many rationalists (see opposite) believe that we are born with ideas already in our minds. According to Plato, these are general ideas, such as "triangle" or "red," which enable us to recognize specific triangles and red things. René Descartes believed that mathematical truths are also innate (or known to us at birth), because statements such as "2 + 2 = 4" are self-evidently true. Plato and Descartes both argued that although we are born with ideas in our minds, experience brings them to consciousness.

TRUTHS OF EXPERIENCE

Empiricism is the belief that we gain knowledge primarily through experience rather than reason. Unlike rationalists (see p.34), empiricists argue that mathematics does not provide us with knowledge but is simply a framework within which to think about the world. The first modern empiricist was John Locke (1632–1704). Following Aristotle, he argued that our senses supply us with knowledge and that reasoning is the process by which we organize our experiences. With its focus on observation, empiricism is the basis of modern science.

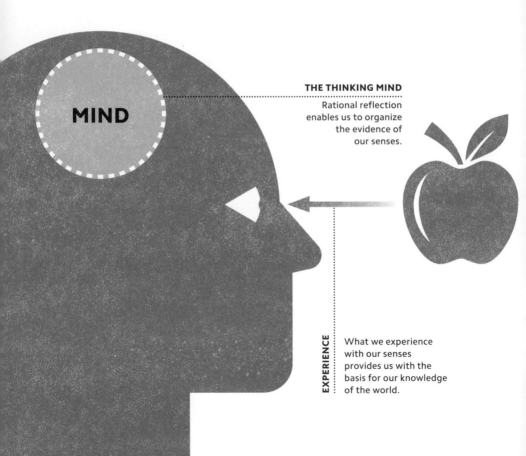

MIND

THE THINKING MIND
Rational reflection enables us to organize the evidence of our senses.

EXPERIENCE
What we experience with our senses provides us with the basis for our knowledge of the world.

No ideas
An unborn child has no ideas. Locke described its mind as a "blank slate" that is waiting to be written on by experience.

Growing ideas
With experience, children form simple ideas, such as "soft" and "dry." These become more complex ideas, such as "toy" and "texture."

ALL KNOWLEDGE IS LEARNED

Empiricists (see opposite) believe that knowledge begins at birth, when we experience the world for the first time. John Locke described the mind as a "blank slate" at birth. He argued that children first have ideas of sensation, which come from the external world through the senses. These develop into more complex ideas of reflection, which come from the mind itself. Although he denied the existence of innate ideas (see p.35), Locke claimed that we do have an innate capacity for reasoning.

ONLY IDEAS EXIST

George Berkeley (1685–1753) agreed with John Locke that people only gain knowledge through perception (see pp.36–37). However, Berkeley argued that because the experience of qualities such as taste and color can vary between people, there is no guarantee that we all perceive the world in the same way. He concluded that reality consists entirely of minds and their ideas—a theory known as subjective idealism—and that there is no justification for believing that the material world exists.

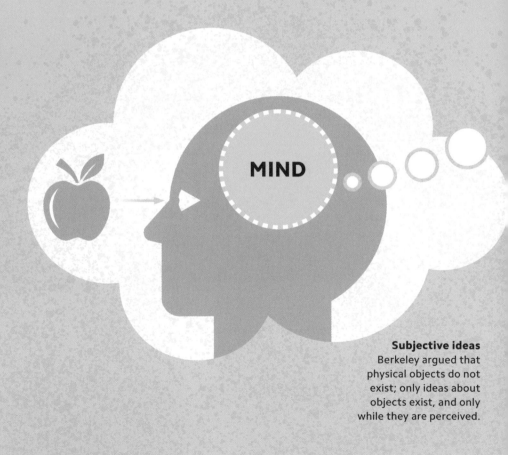

MIND

Subjective ideas
Berkeley argued that physical objects do not exist; only ideas about objects exist, and only while they are perceived.

Fictional self
Hume argued that the self is simply a bundle of impressions about the world—one that only appears to have a fixed identity.

THERE IS NO EXTERNAL WORLD

David Hume (1711–1776) claimed that knowledge is both gained by experience and never certain. According to Hume, humans can never be sure that the external world exists. He agreed with George Berkeley that although people have ideas about the world, they cannot prove that the world exists independently of those ideas (see opposite). Hume proposed that the external world, and the "self" that perceives it, are fictions created by the mind to give coherence to human experiences.

> "The wise man ... proportions his beliefs to the evidence."
> David Hume

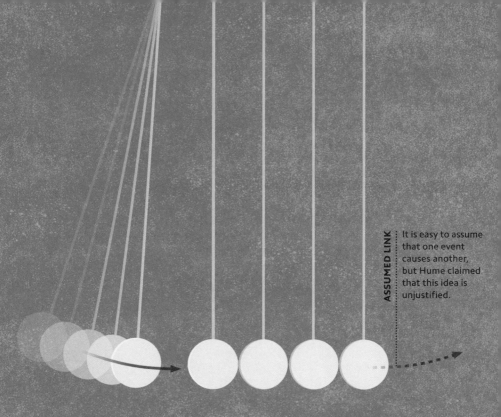

ASSUMED LINK

It is easy to assume that one event causes another, but Hume claimed that this idea is unjustified.

QUESTIONING SCIENCE

David Hume believed that no matter how many times we see one event following another—for example, a ball bouncing when it hits the ground—we can never be justified in making general statements, such as "Balls bounce on the ground." This is because it is always possible that, one day, the second event may not follow the first. He argued that although we experience a "constant conjunction" of events (in other words, events happening together), there is not necessarily a connection between them. Hume's theory questioned the nature of science. The scientific method (see p.150) uses induction, drawing general conclusions about the world from specific observations—precisely in the way that Hume claimed is unjustified.

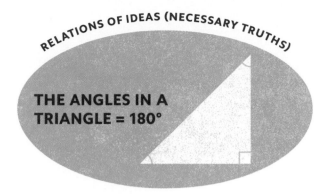

RELATIONS OF IDEAS (NECESSARY TRUTHS)

THE ANGLES IN A TRIANGLE = 180°

HUME'S FORK

Using a distinction known as Hume's Fork, David Hume argued that there are two kinds of truth: "relations of ideas" and "matters of fact." Relations of ideas (for example, "The angles in a triangle add up to 180 degrees") are necessary truths: they are true by definition and therefore cannot be denied without contradiction. Matters of fact (for example, "It is raining") are contingent truths: they are not true by definition, but are true or false depending on their context. According to Hume, only relations of ideas are certain; it is always possible for matters of fact (which include scientific statements) to be wrong (see opposite).

MATTERS OF FACT (CONTINGENT TRUTHS)

IT IS RAINING

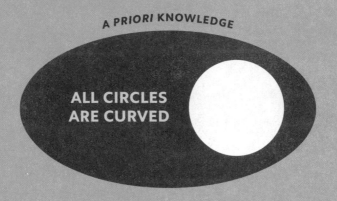

A PRIORI KNOWLEDGE

ALL CIRCLES ARE CURVED

TWO KINDS OF KNOWLEDGE

Immanuel Kant (1724–1804) distinguished *a priori* knowledge, which is known independently of experience, from *a posteriori* knowledge, which is gained through experience. Like David Hume (see p.41), Kant claimed that *a priori* knowledge includes ideas that are true by definition (for example, "All circles are curved"). However, he also believed that it includes some general ideas about the world (for example, "Every event has a cause"). *A posteriori* knowledge includes scientific statements (for example, "The Sun is made of gas") and can only be acquired through experience.

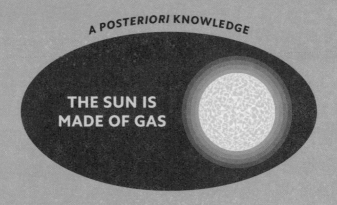

A POSTERIORI KNOWLEDGE

THE SUN IS MADE OF GAS

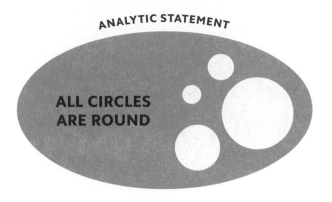

ALL CIRCLES ARE ROUND

TWO KINDS OF STATEMENT

According to Immanuel Kant (see opposite), there are two types of statement. An analytic statement (for example, "All circles are round") is one that is true by definition, so it contains *a priori* knowledge. A synthetic statement (for example, "All planets are round") provides information that goes beyond the definition of a concept, so it contains *a posteriori* knowledge. However, Kant also claimed that there are synthetic *a priori* statements (for example, "Objects have location"), which have to be true, but also do more than merely define a concept.

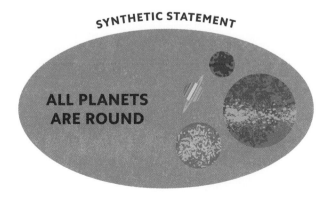

SYNTHETIC STATEMENT

ALL PLANETS ARE ROUND

OUR MINDS SHAPE THE WORLD

Immanuel Kant believed that both rationalism and empiricism (see pp.34–37) were partly true. He argued that although we gain knowledge through experience, our minds are programmed to perceive the world in a particular way. For example, a child grasps the concepts "here" and "now" because it has an innate understanding of the concepts "space" and "time." Kant claimed that we project two innate "intuitions" of space and time onto objects and then interpret them in those terms. He also listed another 12 "categories" that enable us to organize our perceptions of the world. These include the concepts of reality, unity, and existence.

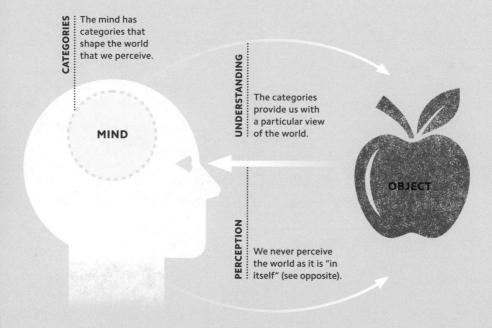

CATEGORIES The mind has categories that shape the world that we perceive.

MIND

UNDERSTANDING The categories provide us with a particular view of the world.

PERCEPTION We never perceive the world as it is "in itself" (see opposite).

OBJECT

THINGS IN THEMSELVES

Immanuel Kant claimed that the world is shaped by our minds—that everything we experience is filtered through our categories of understanding (see opposite). This means that a person looking at an apple does not perceive it as it is "in itself," but rather a representation of it: the actual apple is not knowable. This representation is what Kant called the "phenomenal world," and he contrasted it with the "noumenal world," which is the unknowable world of things in themselves.

THE WORLD IS SPIRIT

Georg Hegel (1770–1831) argued that if the real world cannot be known (see p.45), then there is no reason to say that it exists at all. In a theory known as absolute idealism, he proposed that the world is not divided into thoughts and objects, but that everything is part of a single reality, which he called "*Geist*," or "Spirit." *Geist* is like a universal mind that is continuously evolving through a process that Hegel called the "dialectic" (see opposite). According to Hegel, humans are central to this process: because humans are a part of *Geist*, their discovery that everything is *Geist* is also *Geist*'s own discovery of itself.

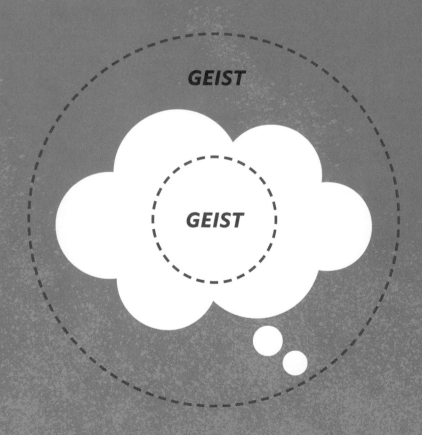

GEIST

GEIST

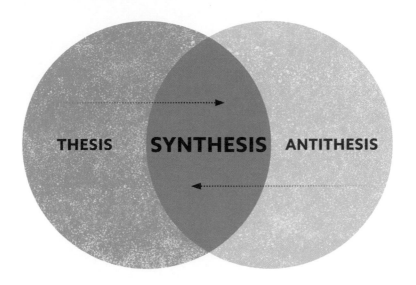

THESIS   **SYNTHESIS**   ANTITHESIS

REALITY IS A PROCESS

Georg Hegel described the process by which *Geist*,
or Spirit, evolves (see opposite) as the "dialectic."
By this, he meant that it was a process in which
an initial idea (a thesis) gives rise to its opposite (an
antithesis), which together form a new, richer idea
(a synthesis). For example, the idea "tyranny" gives
rise to its opposite, "anarchy," and the two form a
synthesis in the idea "law." Hegel argued that, through
the dialectic, *Geist* produces ever more sophisticated
forms of itself. He predicted that *Geist* will one
day reach the Absolute—the time when all its
contradictions are resolved and it returns to the
state it was in at the beginning of the dialectic,
before it "emptied itself into time." Hegel claimed
that the Absolute was near and that history had
therefore run its course.

According to Schopenhauer, the world that we experience is only a representation of the world as it is "in itself."

The world "in itself" is will: an unconscious drive for survival and self-expression.

"The world is my representation."
Arthur Schopenhauer

AN INNER DRIVE

Arthur Schopenhauer (1788–1860) agreed with Immanuel Kant's distinction between the phenomenal and noumenal worlds—that is, between the world as we perceive it to be and the world as it is "in itself" (see p.45). However, unlike Kant, he believed that the noumenal world is knowable. He claimed that the noumenal world is "will," which is a blind, unconscious drive to survive. For Schopenhauer, this drive is present in everything—even in the force of gravity—and is the ultimate source of the world that we experience.

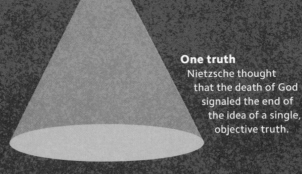

One truth
Nietzsche thought that the death of God signaled the end of the idea of a single, objective truth.

In *The Gay Science*, Friedrich Nietzsche (1844–1900) announced that "God is dead." By this, he meant that the idea of "objective truth"—formerly represented by God—could no longer be rationally justified. Instead, he argued that what we think of as "truth" is simply a fiction that serves particular needs. For example, we believe in free will not because we are free but because we need to hold people accountable for their actions. Known as perspectivism, Nietzsche's theory suggests that because truth is a matter of perspective, there are in fact many truths.

GOD IS DEAD

Many truths
Nietzsche argued that there are many truths, each of which expresses a particular human need.

"God is dead! God remains dead! And we have killed him."
Friedrich Nietzsche

TRUTH AND USEFULNESS

Charles Sanders Peirce (1839–1914) argued that it is impossible to have a complete and accurate understanding of reality. However, he thought that "the truth" can be redefined in terms of the usefulness of ideas, or their practical applications. Known as pragmatism, this idea was developed by William James (1842–1910), who distinguished between facts and truths. For James, facts are simple statements about reality, whereas truths are theories about reality that are not necessarily accurate in terms of how they represent the world but are nevertheless useful for fulfilling a particular purpose.

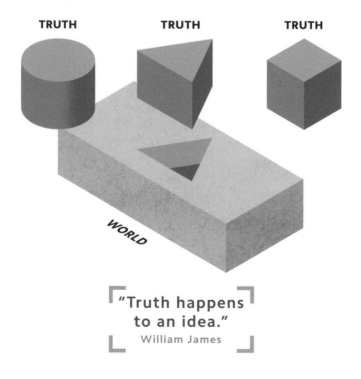

TRUTH TRUTH TRUTH

WORLD

"Truth happens to an idea."
William James

> "Arriving at one goal is the starting point to another."
> John Dewey

IDEAS AS TOOLS

One of the first philosophers to explore pragmatism (see opposite) further was John Dewey (1859–1952). He developed what he called "instrumentalism," which is the view that ideas are not representations of reality, but are tools that either help or hinder us in our lives. He argued that the best ideas are those that enable us to adapt to the world around us.

BE IN

LANG

_____

G AND
UAGE

In the early 20th century, philosophy was increasingly dominated by two schools of thought: the "continental" tradition of mainland Europe and the emerging British "analytic" approach. The philosophers of the continental school continued the work of René Descartes and Immanuel Kant, focusing particularly on questions about the nature of experience. Meanwhile, the philosophers of the analytic school, led by Gottlob Frege and Bertrand Russell, concentrated on analyzing the logical structure of language. Still active today, these two schools offer radically different approaches to philosophy.

> "We let a sign express its sense and designate its denotation."
> Gottlob Frege

Reference
"The morning star" and "the evening star" are two phrases that have the same reference: the planet Venus.

THE EVENING STAR

THE MORNING STAR

Sense
The phrases "the morning star" and "the evening star" have two different senses, or meanings.

WHAT DO WE MEAN?

For centuries, astronomers believed that the phrases "the morning star" and "the evening star" referred to two different stars, when in fact both "stars" were the planet Venus. Gottlob Frege (1848–1925) argued that this example shows that the "sense," or meaning, of a word is not tied to the object to which it refers. Instead, he distinguished between the "sense" of a word and its "reference"—the thing to which it refers. "The morning star" and "the evening star" have the same reference, Venus, but express two different senses, depending on the context of "morning" or "evening."

TAKING LANGUAGE APART

Bertrand Russell (1872–1970) believed that language can be misleading and that the philosopher's role is to analyze its logical structure. For example, he pointed out that the statement "The present king of France is bald" appears to make sense but is clearly not true. However, there is a logical problem: the statement's opposite, "The present king of France is not bald," is also clearly not true. Russell proposed that the first statement makes three claims: that there is a king of France; that there is only one king of France; and that the king of France is bald. In this way, the problem with the statement can be identified: the first of the claims is false, because there is no king of France.

THE PRESENT KING OF FRANCE IS BALD

THERE IS A KING OF FRANCE

THERE IS ONLY ONE KING OF FRANCE

THE KING OF FRANCE IS BALD

Underlying structure
Russell argued that the sentence "The present king of France is bald" is in fact a combination of three separate statements.

THIS SQUARE IS BLUE

SQUARES HAVE FOUR SIDES

TRUTH AND MEANING

A group of 20th-century philosophers known as the Vienna Circle established a school of thought called logical positivism, with the aim of providing a scientific basis for philosophy. They argued that the meaning of a sentence is its method of verification—how it is proven to be true. Factual statements can be verified by observation, and logical statements can be verified with reasoning. Any other kind of statement—such as a statement of aesthetic preference—cannot be verified and is therefore meaningless.

MEANINGLESS STATEMENT

SQUARES ARE BEAUTIFUL

PICTURING THE WORLD

Early in his career, Ludwig Wittgenstein (1889–1951) believed that the function of language is to take "pictures" of the world, which he argued is made up of "facts," or combinations of existing objects. He claimed that a meaningful sentence is one that can be reduced to statements about simple facts, or "atoms" of meaning (for example, "an apple" or "a table"), and that any sentence that fails to represent an observable fact—for example, by expressing a value instead—is therefore meaningless. However, he also believed that works of art can "show" things that cannot be said in a way that he described as "mystical."

THERE'S AN APPLE ON THE TABLE

Making sense
Wittgenstein believed that language mirrors reality, so a meaningful sentence is one that "takes a picture" of the world.

BRICK THAT UP

THIS IS
A BRICK

IT LOOKS
LIKE A
BRICK

One word, many uses

One word, many uses
According to Wittgenstein, the word
"brick" can act like a one-word sentence.
Depending on how it is used, its meaning
could be the name of an object, an order,
a question, a comparison, or a warning.

BRICK

DANGER:
FALLING
BRICK

BRING ME
A BRICK

WOULD YOU
LIKE A BRICK?

THE USE OF WORDS

In his later work, Ludwig Wittgenstein claimed that it
was a mistake to assume that the meaning of a word is an
object that it refers to (see pp.54, 57). He argued instead that
words have countless purposes and that learning to speak
is like learning a series of games. These "language games,"
as he called them, are socially agreed-upon ways of using
words (see opposite), which enable us not only to name
objects, but also to express feelings and influence people. For
Wittgenstein, speaking is a "form of life"—a way of behaving
rather than simply a way of categorizing objects.

PRIVATE LANGUAGE IS IMPOSSIBLE

In Ludwig Wittgenstein's later work, he argued that much of modern philosophy is based on the false assumption that there are things that only individuals can know, in private thoughts—for example, René Descartes' certainty that he alone existed (see p.32). Wittgenstein claimed that such private thoughts are impossible, because thoughts occur in language, and language cannot exist without a community of language speakers (see opposite). He concluded that there is no such thing as private meaning, and that certainty cannot be found in private experience (see p.83).

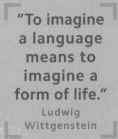

"To imagine a language means to imagine a form of life."
Ludwig Wittgenstein

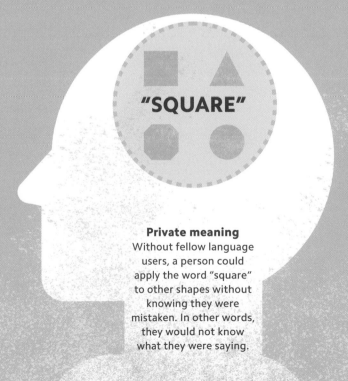

"SQUARE"

Private meaning
Without fellow language users, a person could apply the word "square" to other shapes without knowing they were mistaken. In other words, they would not know what they were saying.

WHO STOLE THE CHALK?

I DID

THE MEANING OF "I"

Ludwig Wittgenstein believed that philosophical problems come from the misuse of language (see p.59). For example, if a teacher asks "Who stole the chalk?" and a pupil says "I did," the pupil uses the word "I" to distinguish herself from the rest of the class. However, when René Descartes claimed, "I think, therefore I am," he used the word "I" to distinguish himself from his body (see p.32). Wittgenstein saw this as an example of language "going on vacation." He argued that when language is used in an "ordinary" way, as by the pupil above, philosophical problems vanish.

I AM NOT MY BODY

"I" in philosophy
Wittgenstein thought that philosophers use words such as "I" in abnormal ways, and in doing so create philosophical problems.

OBSERVATION
Scientists may observe that all of the swans ever seen have been white.

THEORY
Based on observation, scientists may theorize that all swans are white.

EXCEPTION
The theory "All swans are white" is scientific, because the discovery of a black swan would show it to be false.

ARE ALL SWANS WHITE?

Karl Popper (1902–1994) argued that for a theory to be scientific, there have to be conditions under which it can be shown to be false. He used the example of the theory "All swans are white," which is scientific because a single observation of a black swan would disprove it. Popper overturned the traditional idea that scientists have to prove that their theories are true. Instead, he proposed that a theory can only be considered to be scientific if there is a possibility that evidence might exist that proves it false.

CONSCIOUSNESS IS INTENTIONAL

René Descartes (see pp.32–33) and many empiricists (see p.36) claimed that ideas in the mind are like pictures. This raised the question of how such pictures relate to what exists outside the mind. Franz Brentano (1838–1917) undermined this question entirely by arguing that consciousness is "intentional," or always "about" something. In other words, he proposed that objects in the world are not outside of consciousness, but are instead an intrinsic part of it. This enabled philosophers to study consciousness as it is in itself, separately from the question of how ideas relate to reality. Brentano called this study "phenomenology".

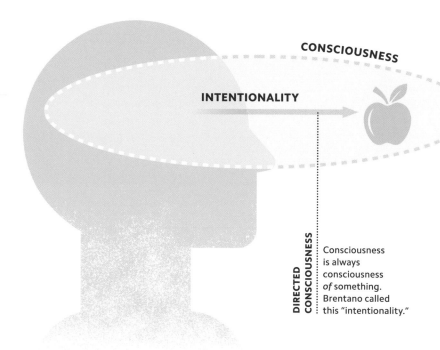

CONSCIOUSNESS

INTENTIONALITY

DIRECTED CONSCIOUSNESS

Consciousness is always consciousness *of* something. Brentano called this "intentionality."

STUDYING CONSCIOUSNESS

People generally assume that an object, such as an apple, exists in the world, but that a thing that someone imagines does not. Edmund Husserl (1859–1938) called these assumptions the "natural attitude." To make phenomenology (see opposite) a more rigorous study of consciousness, he developed a method designed to minimize this attitude. He used the Greek term *"epoché"* (meaning "to bracket") to describe this method, which involves "bracketing out," or ignoring, our natural assumptions about consciousness. Doing so does not reject these assumptions, but it stops them from interfering with the analysis of consciousness itself.

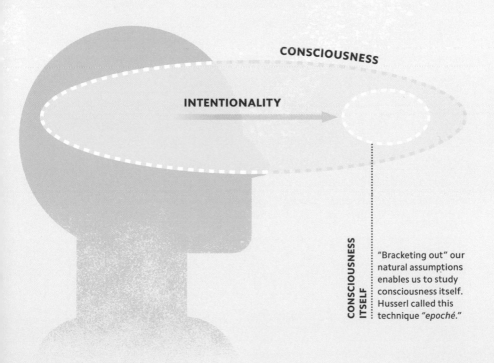

CONSCIOUSNESS

INTENTIONALITY

CONSCIOUSNESS ITSELF

"Bracketing out" our natural assumptions enables us to study consciousness itself. Husserl called this technique *"epoché."*

PAST

TIME

Heidegger argued
that as time passes,
we understand
Being—but we do
so by living rather
than by theorizing.

BEING AND TIME

Martin Heidegger (1889–1976) thought that humans
are continuously directed toward things: that is,
toward physical objects (for example, apple trees) and
especially toward future ends (for example, harvesting
apples). He used the term *"Dasein,"* or "Being-in-the-
world," to describe human beings and argued that
Dasein is "stretched" across time—from the conditions
that existed before the present and into the future.
According to Heidegger, our ability to understand is
similarly stretched; to understand something is not to
form an accurate theory of it, but rather for it already
to be an integral part of our lives. He also claimed that
because *Dasein* is stretched across time, time itself is
the means by which Being can be understood.

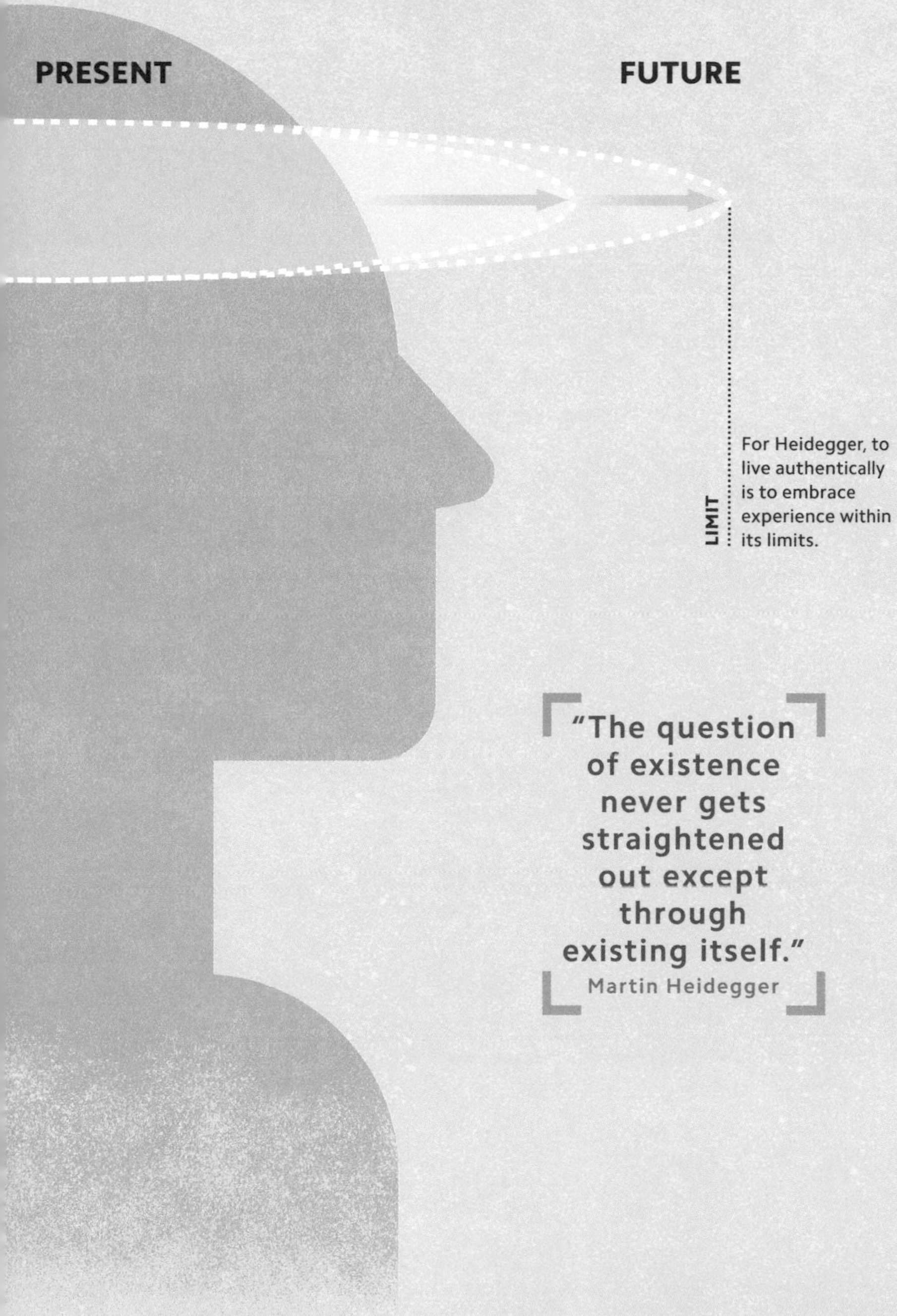

PRESENT   FUTURE

LIMIT

For Heidegger, to
live authentically
is to embrace
experience within
its limits.

"The question
of existence
never gets
straightened
out except
through
existing itself."
Martin Heidegger

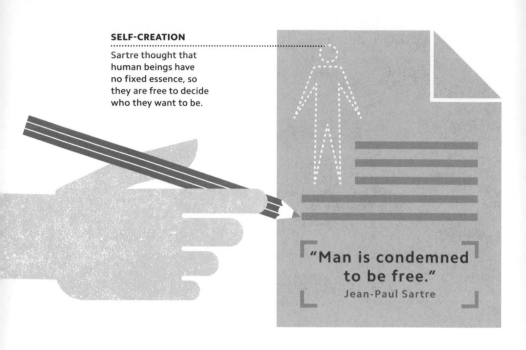

SELF-CREATION
Sartre thought that
human beings have
no fixed essence, so
they are free to decide
who they want to be.

"Man is condemned
to be free."
Jean-Paul Sartre

ABSURDITY AND ANXIETY

Jean-Paul Sartre (1905–1980) claimed that humans are
different from all other things in two ways. First, he argued
that humans do not have a fixed essence, or purpose, as
Aristotle had claimed (see pp.20–22). Lacking an essence,
human existence is therefore "absurd." Second, he argued
that humans are not subject to natural laws, such as the law
of cause and effect. Instead, they are free at every moment,
although realizing this causes them "anxiety." Sartre argued
that a human being can only be truly human—or, as he said,
be "authentic"—by learning to live with absurdity and anxiety.

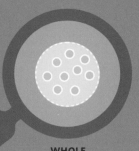

WHOLE

General study
Understanding the
whole of a thing helps
us understand its parts.

UNDERSTANDING

PART

UNDERSTANDING
IS CIRCULAR

Hermeneutics is the study of understanding. Its
key principle is that understanding has a circular
structure. For example, to ask a question, we
must already know something about the
answer—because we know that there is
a question to ask. Likewise, to understand
the whole of something first requires an
understanding of its parts, while to understand
a part requires an understanding of the whole.
Understanding is therefore an ongoing, circular
process—one in which we refine our assumptions
and so change our picture of the world.

UNDERSTANDING

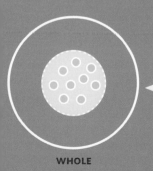

Detailed study
Understanding the parts
of a thing helps us
understand the whole.

WHOLE

PART

DEFINING FEMININITY

As an existentialist (see p.66), Simone de Beauvoir (1908–1986) was supposed to believe that people are free to become anything they like. But de Beauvoir argued that women do not have absolute freedom. She claimed that they are limited by a patriarchal culture, in which men are subjects—free to act and see—whereas women are objects to be seen and acted upon. This culture encourages women to behave in prescribed "feminine" ways. As girls grow up, they internalize their role as object and can become oppressed by it. For de Beauvoir, women are formed by society and not solely by their choices.

INCREASING SOCIALIZATION

Baby
A baby known to be female is often said to be "pretty" rather than "strong" or "energetic."

Infant
As she develops, an infant female is encouraged to behave like a "little girl."

Youth
As the female reaches puberty, she is socialized further and learns to be "modest."

Adult
The adult female is fully socialized to act "like a woman" and to defer to the male.

GENDER IS A PERFORMANCE

Drawing on Simone de Beauvoir's ideas (see opposite), Judith Butler (1956–) argued that gender is not an internal reality or a natural state, but something that a person does. In Butler's view, gender is created by repeatedly performing acts that are considered masculine or feminine: the way a person walks, talks, and behaves leads them to be seen as either male or female. Such acts follow a script that is taught from birth, and roles are enforced by strong social norms. Because gender identities are performed, they can be subverted by behaving in ways that challenge traditional gender roles. For Butler, even the body is not simply female or male: sex itself is shaped by cultural expectations about gender.

THE DEATH OF MAN

SUPREME BEING

Enlightenment humanists believed that human beings had almost God-like powers of reason. According to Foucault, no such powers are possible.

During the Enlightenment (17th–19th centuries), European philosophers believed that human beings are essentially rational and are capable of knowing the truth about the world and themselves. Michel Foucault (1926–1984) disagreed with this idea, which is known as humanism. According to Foucault, the humanist view of "man" is nearing its end, "like a face drawn in the sand at the edge of the sea." He argued that what we call "reason" and "truth" change over time: there is no fixed truth about humanity for us to find, but we *can* learn to think and act in new ways.

MEANING IS DIFFERENCE

Structuralism, as developed by Ferdinand de Saussure (1857–1913), rejects the view of the empiricists (see p.36) that language works by referring to things in the world. Instead, structuralists argue that language is a system of signs that exists independently of both the mind and physical reality. For example, the meaning of the word "cat" is not what it refers to in the world, but its difference from other words. These differences form structures of meaning that enable people to communicate and agree (or disagree) on what is true.

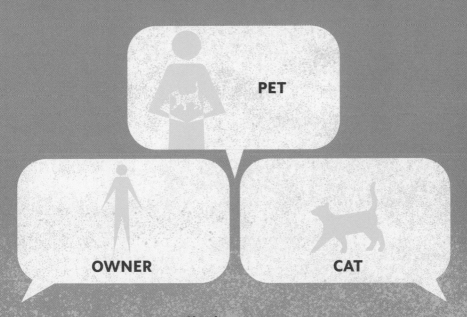

PET

OWNER

CAT

Simple structure
In this example, the word "pet" builds
on the words "owner" and "cat" to form
a simple structure of meaning.

MEANING IS NOT FIXED

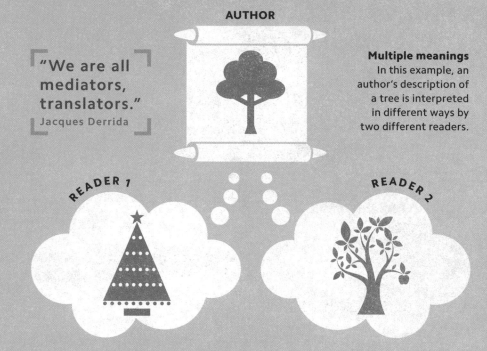

AUTHOR

"We are all mediators, translators."
Jacques Derrida

Multiple meanings
In this example, an author's description of a tree is interpreted in different ways by two different readers.

READER 1

READER 2

Structuralists claim that meaning relies on structures of differences between words (see p.71). However, poststructuralists argue that this claim ignores the role that tone, intention, and context play in communication. They also accuse structuralists of assuming that the meanings of words such as "structure" and "language" are fixed independently of the structures they are supposed to rely on. According to poststructuralists, the meanings of words are much "looser" than structuralists claim—so much so that we should abandon the idea that truth, as expressed in language, refers to reality.

THERE IS NO OUTSIDE-TEXT

Jacques Derrida (1930–2004) was one of the best-known poststructuralist philosophers (see opposite). He criticized philosophers of the Western tradition for assuming that fixed reference points for truth could ever be "present." Derrida thought that this assumption was part of an illusion that he called the "metaphysics of presence." He used the word "deconstruction" to describe the process of exposing this illusion. Using the example of written texts, Derrida argued that because the meanings of words always depend on the meanings of other words, it is impossible to have a complete understanding of them. As he put it, there could never be an "outside-text" that could be present and reveal the full meaning of any text.

LOCAL TRUTHS

In his book *The Postmodern Condition*, Jean-François Lyotard (1924–1998) defined postmodernism as an attitude of "incredulity toward metanarratives." By this, he meant that we can no longer believe in the grand stories that we once used to make sense of the world—for example, the biblical tale of creation, the Marxist account of history (see pp.128–129), or the progress of science. In the absence of such narratives, all events are understood in many different ways, which Lyotard called "micronarratives." In his view, justice is more important than truth: we must ensure that micronarratives are heard and not immediately silenced by a supposed "universal" narrative.

Thomas Kuhn (1922–1996) argued that, under normal circumstances, scientists have a shared understanding, or "paradigm," of how the world works. However, every now and then, when evidence against an accepted scientific theory builds up, science suffers a crisis. According to Kuhn, such crises can only be resolved when scientists are able to look at the world in new ways—or, as he put it, when scientific thinking undergoes a "paradigm shift." One such shift occurred when physicists stopped thinking of time and space as being the same for all observers (as Newton had argued) and started seeing them as being relative to each observer (as Einstein argued). Kuhn claimed that science only progresses by means of such paradigm shifts.

SCIENCE ADAPTS

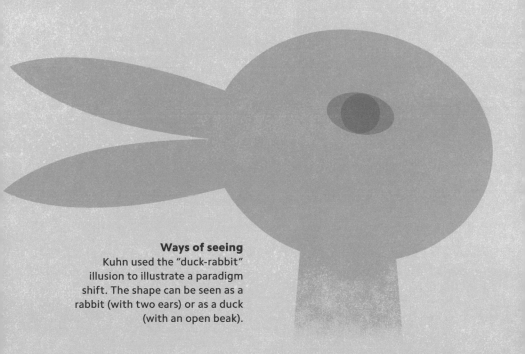

Ways of seeing
Kuhn used the "duck-rabbit" illusion to illustrate a paradigm shift. The shape can be seen as a rabbit (with two ears) or as a duck (with an open beak).

MIND
MATT

A N D

E R

The philosophy of mind focuses on the nature of consciousness and the relationship between the mind and the body. Philosophers who study it are generally either dualists (who believe that the mind and the body are different kinds of thing) or monists (who believe that only one kind of thing exists—either matter, mind, or something of which both matter and mind are aspects). Other philosophers argue that the "mind/body problem"— that of whether the mind and the body are separate, and how they interact—is unsolvable. Still others claim that the concept of "mind" should be abandoned altogether.

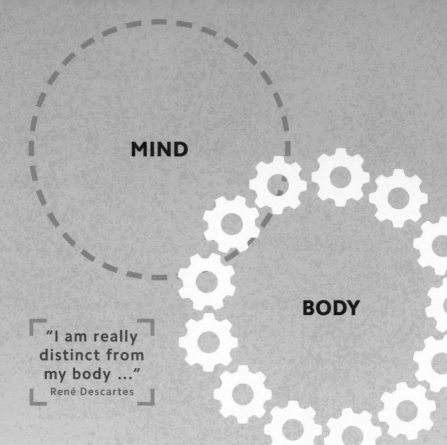

MIND

BODY

"I am really distinct from my body ..."
René Descartes

MIND AND BODY

René Descartes claimed that humans are made of two substances: a material body and an immaterial mind (see p.33). He did so because he believed that although the universe runs like clockwork, humans are uniquely free. However, his claim raised the question of how the mind and the body interact. Descartes imagined that the mind "commingles" with the body in the pineal gland of the brain, which he described as "the place in which all our thoughts are formed." His theory, known as dualism, is popular today, but there are still questions about how the mind can interact with the body (see opposite).

Physicalists claim that the idea that the mind is separate from the body (see opposite) is flawed. They argue that physical objects can interact with each other because they have location and mass, but because an immaterial mind has neither, it cannot interact with the body. Physicalists believe that the world is causally complete—that is, that a physical description of the brain and the senses describes all that there is to know about what causes events in the mind. For this reason, Gilbert Ryle (1900–1976) called the dualists' concept of mind a "ghost in the machine"—in other words, an illusion with no influence over the body.

THE WORLD IS CAUSALLY COMPLETE

MIND

WORLD

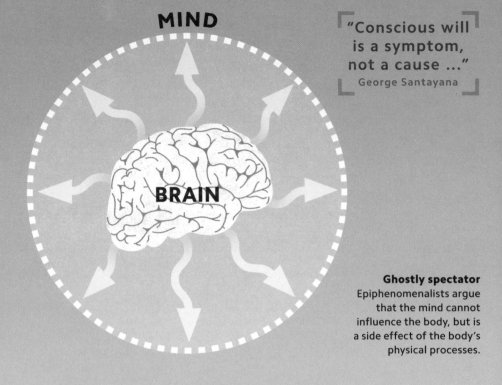

MIND

BRAIN

Ghostly spectator
Epiphenomenalists argue that the mind cannot influence the body, but is a side effect of the body's physical processes.

THE HELPLESS MIND

Many dualists (see p.78) accept that because the mind is not physical, it cannot interact with the body. According to this view, the mind is a helpless epiphenomenon, or by-product, of the brain. T. H. Huxley (1825–1895), who defended this idea, compared the mind to a steam train's whistle—a device that is powered by steam produced by the engine but plays no role in moving the train. Epiphenomenalists argue that if the mind has no power over the body, then free will is an illusion. Recent scientific research seems to support this idea; some studies have shown that there is significant activity in a person's brain up to two seconds before that person is aware of making a decision.

HUMAN OR ZOMBIE?

Many philosophers argue that if knowledge is based on perception, then we can never be sure that other people are conscious—because we can only ever perceive their bodies and not their minds. We assume that other people are conscious and have inner lives like ours, but they might, in fact, be zombies that simply act like human beings. Although we believe that other people have minds, because they react to the world as we do (for example, by crying out in pain or laughing), their reactions could be purely mechanical and not involve a mind at all.

Ourselves
We know that we are conscious because we have thoughts, feelings, and sensations.

Others
We cannot perceive other people's thoughts, so we cannot be certain that those other people are conscious.

Different perspectives
We cannot be sure how other people see an apple, but we know how it appears to us. Some philosophers think that qualia such as this are all that we can know for certain.

IMMEDIATE EXPERIENCE

Qualia are the qualities of immediate experience—such as the redness of a rose or the feeling of pain. They are not descriptions of those qualities (which can be shared), but the qualities themselves, which can only be known as they are experienced. The existence of qualia has been used as evidence that the theory of materialism (see p.30) is mistaken. For example, dualists (see p.78) argue that a physical account of hearing explains how sound affects the ear but not what it is like to experience the sound of music. According to this view, materialism ignores the fact that people are subjects of experience and have private, "inner," perspectives.

QUESTIONING QUALIA

Ludwig Wittgenstein questioned the concept of qualia (see opposite). In a thought experiment, he imagined a community in which everyone has a box in which they keep something that they call a "beetle," which no one else is allowed to look at. Wittgenstein claimed that, in public, the word "beetle" could mean "whatever we keep in our boxes," but it could never refer to any specific thing—because there would be no agreement on what a "beetle" is. However, he argued that, in private, the word would also be meaningless, because the meanings of words are shared, public conventions (see p.60). He concluded that qualia are like "beetles"—things that can either be spoken about (so are not private) or have no meaning at all.

I'M THINKING ABOUT MY BEETLE

BODY LANGUAGE

Some philosophers, known as behaviorists, argue that the question of how the mind interacts with the body (see p.78) rises from a confusion about language. They claim that dualists wrongly assume that people have two kinds of traits: physical traits, which relate to their bodies (for example, their height), and mental traits, which relate to their minds (for example, their intelligence). Instead, according to behaviorists, all human traits are either physical or *behavioral* in nature: people are "clever" or "happy" because they behave in specific ways, not because their minds have the traits of "cleverness" or "happiness." Behaviorists argue that what dualists call "mental attributes" are simply tendencies to behave in a certain way.

YOU'RE SAD

IS THAT WHAT YOU CALL IT?

Sad behavior
Behaviorists argue that we learn words such as "sad" by associating them with certain kinds of behavior.

> "Minds are not bits of
> clockwork; they are just
> bits of not-clockwork."
> Gilbert Ryle

MENTAL SPACE

For Ryle, the illusion that we have a space in which we "think" comes from the idea that the mind is an immaterial "thing."

DUALISM IS WRONG

WHY IS THAT?

INTERNAL SPEECH

In Ryle's view, thinking involves having imaginary conversations in which problems are analyzed and solved.

Imaginary speaking

Gilbert Ryle argued that thinking is also a behavior—a form of imaginary speaking. He also claimed that because speaking is a public activity, there is nothing necessarily private about our thoughts.

BELIEFS

DESIRES

INTENTIONS

THE MIND
IS THE BRAIN

In recent years, physicalists (see p.79) have argued that mental states are the same as brain states. For example, U. T. Place (1924–2000) compared the terms "sensation" and "brain state" to "lightning" and "electrical discharge" and claimed that, in each case, they refer to the same physical thing—one is simply a more formal way of describing the other. He argued that in day-to-day life, we talk informally about emotions and intentions, but that an accurate explanation of consciousness should only refer to the brain and brain processes.

"Two events that always occur together at the same time in the same place ... are not two events but the same event."
Edwin G. Boring

THE MIND AS MYTH

Some physicalists (see opposite) argue that the concepts that we usually use to explain human behavior are so misleading that they should be abandoned in favor of scientific terms. Known as eliminative materialists, they claim that ordinary language uses mythical ideas—such as beliefs, desires, and intentions—that fail to explain how human beings really work. According to eliminative materialists, the biggest myth of all is the mind itself, which they argue is nothing more than a network of physical processes.

Mythical entities
Some physicalists claim that the "self," like a god, is an imaginary being that does not explain human behavior.

Statements of reality
Eliminative materialists think that the words "I am angry" should be replaced with a statement about the brain.

ZEUS IS ANGRY

A STORM IS HERE

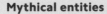

I AM ANGRY

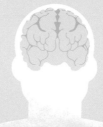

A BRAIN IS DOING "X"

CAN A MACHINE THINK?

Some philosophers focus on what the mind does rather than what it is. Known as functionalists, they argue that if a human being and a machine can perform the same cognitive tasks, then they should be considered equally intelligent. For functionalists, human mental states—such as thinking or believing—are like software that runs on the hardware of the brain.

Assessing intelligence
Functionalists believe that judging a being's intelligence means judging its behavior rather than its physical make-up.

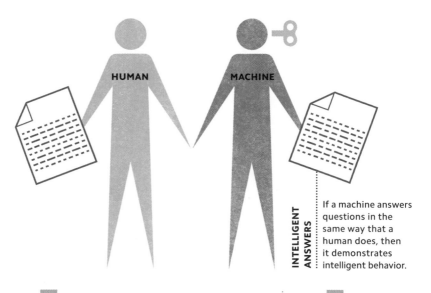

HUMAN

MACHINE

INTELLIGENT ANSWERS
If a machine answers questions in the same way that a human does, then it demonstrates intelligent behavior.

"Why may we not say that all automata ... have an artificial life?"
Thomas Hobbes

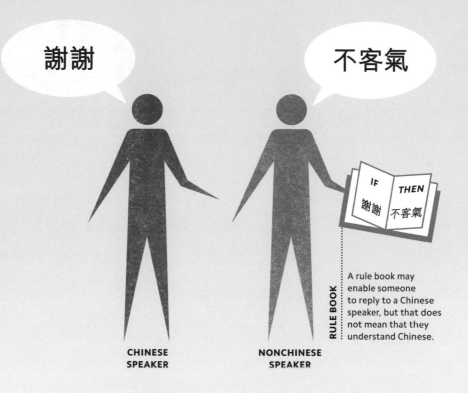

A rule book may enable someone to reply to a Chinese speaker, but that does not mean that they understand Chinese.

CHINESE SPEAKER

NONCHINESE SPEAKER

RULE BOOK

HUMAN UNDERSTANDING

John Searle (1932–) thought that functionalists (see opposite) ignore the main difference between humans and machines: that humans understand, but machines do not. He claimed that while humans have languages with both syntax (grammatical structure) and semantics (meaning), machines only have instructions, which are equivalent to syntax alone. He likened the difference to someone who understands Chinese, as opposed to someone who follows a rule book for speaking Chinese.

COGS IN A HIGHER MACHINE

Baruch Spinoza (1632–1677) argued that just as height and color are two attributes of physical objects, mind and matter are two attributes of an underlying substance—one that he referred to as both "God" and "nature." Spinoza did not believe in an otherworldly creator, but in a God that exists in all things, and he thought that mind and matter are the two aspects of God that humans understand. He believed that just as the height of an object does not determine its color, matter does not determine the mind, or vice versa— the two operate in parallel.

AN UNSOLVABLE MYSTERY

Mysterians claim that consciousness is a mystery that may never be solved. Following C. S. Peirce (see p.50), they distinguish between problems, which are in principle solvable, and mysteries, which cannot be solved because they lie outside the scope of human understanding. They argue that the cognitive scope of an organism (what it is able to understand) is decided by its biological needs, and that just as chimpanzees do not need to understand astronomy, humans do not need to understand the nature of consciousness.

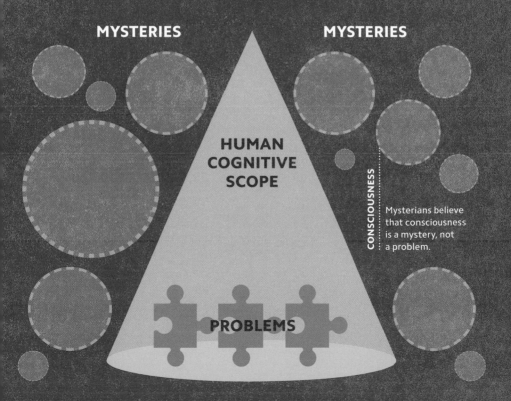

MYSTERIES

MYSTERIES

HUMAN
COGNITIVE
SCOPE

CONSCIOUSNESS

Mysterians believe that consciousness is a mystery, not a problem.

PROBLEMS

RIGH
WRON

T A N D
G

Ethics is the branch of philosophy that concerns moral
values. Its key questions include "How should we behave?"
and "How do we know that our moral values are true?"
In answering these questions, philosophers fall into
two main groups: consequentialists, who argue that
the morality of an action depends on its outcome (for
example, Jeremy Bentham), and deontologists, who claim
that the morality of an action depends on whether it
follows moral laws (for example, Immanuel Kant). Ethicists
also examine the meaning of moral concepts, particularly
the concepts of "good," "bad," "evil," and "virtue."

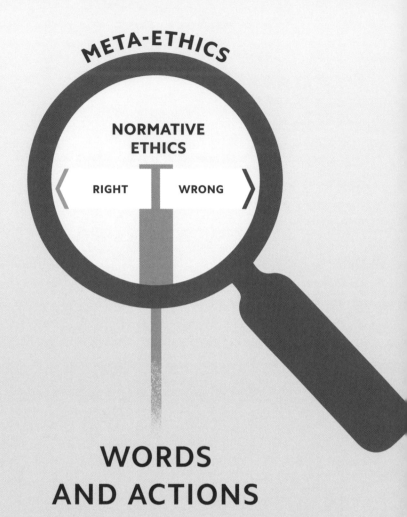

META-ETHICS

NORMATIVE
ETHICS

RIGHT   WRONG

WORDS
AND ACTIONS

Ethics is broadly divided into two major fields: meta-ethics and
normative ethics. Meta-ethics is the more theoretical of the
two. It explores the nature of moral concepts, such as "good"
and "bad," and asks how we are able to differentiate between
right and wrong. Normative ethics, on the other hand, asks the
more practical question, "How should we behave?" It looks at
ways in which we can judge the morality of our actions and
tries to find ethical rules that we can live by.

THE VIRTUOUS LIFE

DEFICIENCY   EXCESS

GOLDEN MEAN

Virtue ethics identifies and examines the human traits that are considered to be virtuous (morally good) and to characterize a virtuous person. These include qualities such as honesty, justice, and generosity. Virtue ethicists also study the nature and definition of virtue, what it means in practice, and how a person can become virtuous. For example, the Ancient Greek philosophers claimed that the goal of a virtuous person is to live a "good life": a life that is fulfilling because it is lived virtuously. Aristotle argued that one of the characteristics of this good life is moderation, which involves finding the "Golden Mean" between deficiency (too little) and excess (too much).

"... it is our choice of good or evil that determines our character, not our opinion about good or evil."

Aristotle

NIRVANA

REINCARNATION

Buddhists believe that if they stray from the principles of the path, they will be reborn into a harder life that is further away from *nirvana*.

Eight principles
The eight aspects of the path are right mindfulness, right action, right concentration, right livelihood, right effort, right intention, right understanding, and right speech.

THE EIGHTFOLD PATH

Buddhism is an ancient religion that originated in India. One of its central ideas is *samsara*, or reincarnation: a repeating cycle of birth, death, and rebirth that can be escaped by leading a good life. Siddhartha Gautama (c.563–483 BCE), venerated as the Buddha, set out the path for a good life, based on eight aspects of living. His followers, known as Buddhists, believe that people can eventually overcome *samsara* by practicing eight principles. The end goal for Buddhists is not heaven, but *nirvana*, a state of not-being and a release from all worldly attachments.

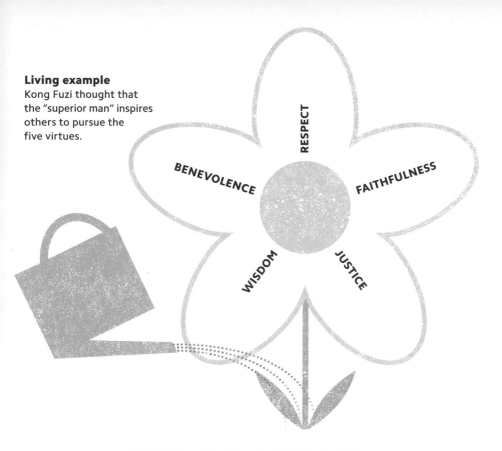

Living example
Kong Fuzi thought that the "superior man" inspires others to pursue the five virtues.

RESPECT

BENEVOLENCE

FAITHFULNESS

WISDOM

JUSTICE

FIVE CONSTANT VIRTUES

Kong Fuzi (551–479 BCE), also known as Confucius, dismissed the idea that virtue is divinely given to a particular social class. Instead, he held that it could be nurtured in everyone in a society founded on what he called the "five constant virtues." For Kong Fuzi, the fundamental virtue is benevolence, which is expressed in the Golden Rule: "Do not do to others what you do not desire for yourself." The second virtue is justice or righteousness; the third is faithfulness or integrity; the fourth wisdom; and the fifth respect, especially for tradition.

A MORAL OUTCOME

Consequentialism is the belief that the moral worth of an action is determined by its outcome rather than whether it conforms to conventional standards or rules of morality. This approach to moral philosophy gained ground in Renaissance Europe during the 15th and 16th centuries, and became the foundation of Jeremy Bentham's utilitarianism (see p.102). Taken to its extremes, as it was by political philosopher Niccolò Machiavelli (1469–1527), consequentialism promotes the idea that "the end justifies the means."

"Every advantage in the past is judged in the light of the final issue."
Demosthenes

GOOD OUTCOME

BAD OUTCOME

A MORAL LAW

The idea that there are moral laws that define what is morally correct, and that it is our duty to follow them regardless of the consequences, is known as deontology. Many deontologists argue that moral laws are like natural laws or mathematical principles and that breaking them is therefore unnatural or irrational. The best-known supporter of deontology in modern ethics is Immanuel Kant, whose idea of the categorical imperative (see p.106) opposed the consequentialist ethics of his time.

THE PLEASURE PRINCIPLE

PAIN

PLEASURE

Hedonism is the idea that pleasure is what determines well-being and that whatever promotes pleasure is therefore morally good. For hedonists, finding pleasure by satisfying desires and appetites is the highest good in life. Because the opposite of pleasure is pain or suffering, the avoidance of these is also good. Hedonism had its origins in the work of Democritus (see p.17) and Aristippus of Cyrene (c.435–c.356 BCE). The idea that pleasure and pain are the primary factors in determining morality can also be found in utilitarianism (see pp.102–103).

TRANQUILITY

Epicureanism
Epicurus defined happiness as a state
of tranquility that is reached by being
free of pain and anxiety—especially
the fear of death. For Epicurus, this
type of happiness was the aim
of a good life.

HAPPY IS THE SAME AS GOOD

In Ancient Greece, moral philosophers aimed to enable
people to live a "good life," meaning one that is both
virtuous and happy. For hedonists (see opposite), these
two concepts were effectively identical. They claimed that
if happiness is the result of moral goodness, then whatever
causes happiness is morally good. One hedonist, Epicurus
(341–270 BCE), founded his own school of thought on the
same principles: it was known as Epicureanism. He argued
that happiness is the aim of a good life, but—unlike
other hedonists—he thought that happiness is found
in tranquility rather than the pursuit of pleasure.

FEAR

THE GREATEST GOOD

During the 18th century, some British philosophers supported the belief that the goodness of an action can be judged by its outcomes (see p.98). Jeremy Bentham (1748–1832), in particular, thought that actions are morally justified by the amount of pleasure or pain they cause. He proposed a formula for calculating the "utility" of actions (the extent to which they have pleasurable or painful outcomes), arguing that the best course of action is the one that leads to the greatest happiness for the greatest number of people. This school of thought is known as utilitarianism.

> "The greatest happiness of the greatest number is the foundation of morals and legislation."
> Jeremy Bentham

Act utilitarianism
In Bentham's view, the utility of each action can be measured by examining its outcomes—that is, by considering the number of people affected and the amount of pleasure or pain they feel. This is known as "act utilitarianism."

THREE PEOPLE MAXIMUM

Rule utilitarianism
It is not always possible to weigh the potential outcomes of an action; decisions often have to be made with limited information. To overcome this, rule utilitarianism suggests following general rules instead of measuring the utility of each action individually.

THE GAP BETWEEN "IS" AND "OUGHT"

FACTS

VALUES

David Hume disagreed with the idea that ethical principles are based on an objective moral law (see p.106). He believed that reason is "the slave of the passions" and claimed that we decide what is good or bad based on our emotions, then use rational thinking to justify our decisions. Because of this, he argued that there is an unbridgeable gap between statements of fact and statements of value—including ethical value. In other words, we cannot know what "ought" to be the case just by knowing what "is" the case.

> "The rules of morality are not conclusions of our reason."
> David Hume

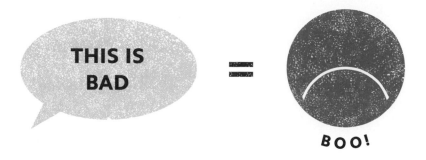

THE BOO-HOORAY THEORY

Subjectivism is the view that moral statements are based on subjective feeling rather than rational thinking. According to subjectivists, our moral values are expressions of feeling rather than statements of fact; for example, when we say "Killing is wrong," we are expressing our feeling that killing should not be done. Likewise, moral codes imposed on us by external authorities, such as "Thou shalt not kill," simply describe what those authorities believe to be acceptable behavior.

Emotivism, or the "boo-hooray theory," is similar to subjectivism. Emotivists argue that the words "good" and "bad" do not have literal meanings and are instead no more than expressions of approval or disapproval—the equivalent of making the sounds "hooray!" or "boo!"

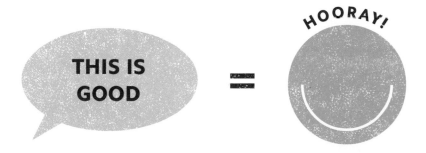

ONE RULE FOR ALL

Immanuel Kant believed that there is a moral law (see p.99) and that it can be discovered by using reason. He called this law the "categorical imperative," which means that it is universally true and that everyone must therefore act upon it. The categorical imperative states that people must act in such a way that they would be willing for their actions to be universal laws—in other words, willing for everyone to do as they did. Kant claimed that failing to act in this way would be irrational. He also argued that actions that are taken to achieve a specific goal (see p.98), rather than to follow the moral law, cannot be ethically justified.

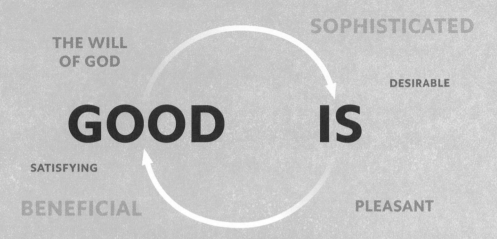

THE WILL
OF GOD

SOPHISTICATED

DESIRABLE

GOOD IS

SATISFYING

BENEFICIAL

PLEASANT

"If I am asked 'What is good?' my
answer is that good is good, and
that is the end of the matter."
G.E. Moore

GOOD IS ONLY GOOD

G. E. Moore (1873–1958) claimed that the word "good"
cannot be defined in terms of any other concept, such as
"pleasant" or "desirable." He argued that although things
that please us are considered good, it is not true that the
word "good" therefore means "that which pleases us."
Likewise, we may say that pleasure is good, but that does not
mean that goodness and pleasure are the same thing. Moore
believed that being pleasant or desirable is a natural property
(a characteristic, like roundness or softness) but that being
good is a non-natural property that cannot be seen, touched,
or simplified. He argued that we recognize goodness
instinctively, and that by defining it, we commit the
"naturalistic fallacy" of confusing it with a natural property.

GOOD

VALUES ARE UNIVERSAL

Some philosophers argue that morality is objective (factual) and that its rules can be discovered, in the same way as the laws of nature. Morality is therefore independent of human thought or activity and is universal. (It applies to everyone in the world at all times.) Whatever is objectively shown to be morally good (for example, "justice" or "charity") is always good, and whatever is shown to be bad (for example, "greed" and "theft") is always bad. Moral universalism, as this belief is known, promotes the idea that a universal ethical theory can be built on objective moral truths.

BAD

GOOD

VALUES ARE SUBJECTIVE

In contrast to moral universalists (see opposite), moral relativists argue that morality is a human construct. This means that it is subjective (a matter of opinion) rather than objective; what is regarded in one context as good may be bad in another context. As evidence of this, relativists point to differences in moral codes between cultures. For example, some cultures today find the consumption of alcohol immoral, but other cultures find it acceptable. Moral relativism promotes the idea that our moral principles are shaped by culture rather than by moral facts.

BAD

FATE OR FREE CHOICE?

Generally, people believe that they have free will:
the ability to choose what to do out of a range of
possibilities. Many philosophers defend this idea, but
others, known as hard determinists, claim that free will
is an illusion. Hard determinists argue that because every
event has a cause, all human actions are predetermined
by past events. A third group of philosophers, known
as soft determinists, argue that free will is compatible
with determinism. According to this view, people have
a degree of freedom, but their decisions are based on
personality traits that are either genetically inherited
or determined by their environment.

Soft determinism
People can choose between a limited number of actions. However, their choices are determined by their characters, which are shaped by biological and environmental factors.

"Man can do what he wills, but he cannot will what he wills."
Arthur Schopenhauer

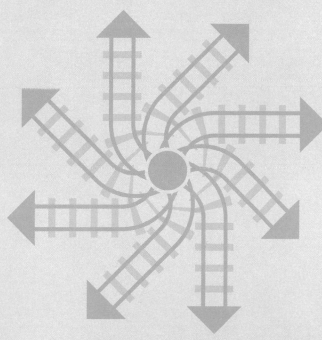

Free will
When faced with a choice, people can do as they wish, because their decisions are not predetermined. Because people have free will, all courses of action are always open to them.

THE ORIGIN OF MORAL VALUES

Friedrich Nietzsche believed that much of modern thinking about morality was outdated. He claimed that our moral values developed at a time when societies were divided into masters and slaves. What he called "slave morality" is religious in nature and emphasizes being humble for the sake of being rewarded in the next life. By contrast, "master morality" is not religious and emphasizes power and achievement in this life. For Nietzsche, now that "God is dead" (see p.49), people are free to choose their own, life-affirming values.

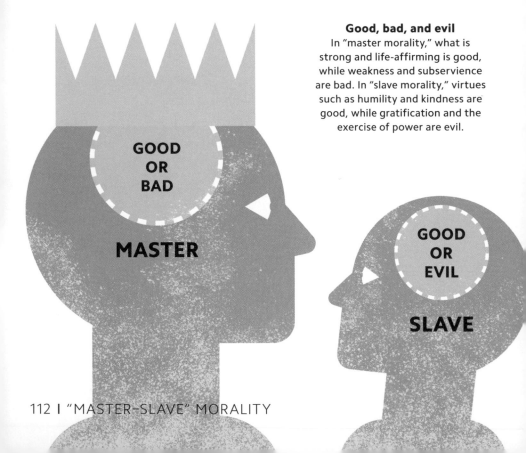

Good, bad, and evil
In "master morality," what is strong and life-affirming is good, while weakness and subservience are bad. In "slave morality," virtues such as humility and kindness are good, while gratification and the exercise of power are evil.

GOOD OR BAD

MASTER

GOOD OR EVIL

SLAVE

The will to power
To Nietzsche, conventional morality is repressive and restricts our natural urges and instincts. These are manifestations of what he calls the "will to power," which drives us to success.

"Become who you are!"
Friedrich Nietzsche

BEYOND GOOD AND EVIL

Friedrich Nietzsche encouraged modern society to abandon "slave morality" (see opposite) and argued that people can choose their own moral values, because their actions should not be thought of in terms of "good" and "evil." He proposed that people are free to live life to the fullest and satisfy their inner needs and desires rather than follow a moral code imposed upon them by others. Nietzsche's term *Übermensch* (or "superman") describes a person who creates their own morality by moving "beyond good and evil."

Pulling a lever will redirect the trolley—an act that will kill one person but save five lives.

MORAL CHOICE

RUNAWAY TROLLEY

A trolley is hurtling down a track with five people in its path.

To highlight the problems of moral choice, Philippa Foot (1920–2010) devised a thought experiment known as the Trolley Problem. It sets up a moral dilemma in which a runaway trolley will kill five people if it is left on its present course. A person standing nearby can pull a lever to divert the trolley onto a side track, where only one person will be killed. If they act, they are responsible for a death; but are they responsible for the five deaths that will occur if they do nothing? For Foot, there is no simple answer to this question.

REAL-WORLD ETHICS

Applied ethics examines the relationship between ethical principles and real-life situations. It looks for common ground between different ethical theories and questions whether some ethical principles can ever be applied consistently. For example, people from different ethical traditions may agree that certain actions are wrong but disagree on why they are wrong. On the other hand, everyone may agree that society should treat people fairly, but individuals may disagree on which type of society best achieves this (see pp.136–137). Applied ethics tries to find agreement, particularly in fields such as politics, economics, technology, and medicine.

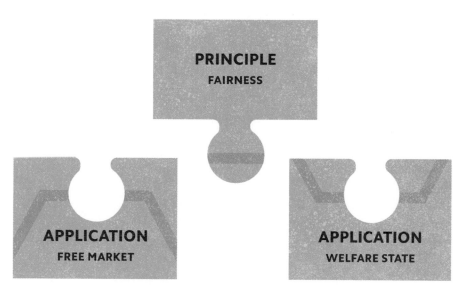

Principle and applications
The principle that society should treat people fairly can be used to justify both a free-market economy (see p.127) and a welfare state, which provides support for the disadvantaged.

THE SUFFERING OF ANIMALS

Early Western philosophers, including Aristotle, believed that there is a hierarchy of living things, ranging from plants, through "lower" animals (such as worms), and then "higher" animals (such as apes), to humans. They claimed that humans are superior because they alone have the ability to reason, and that we should therefore prioritize humans when making moral decisions. Jeremy Bentham, a utilitarian (see p.102), challenged this view. He asked whether animals can suffer and suggested that if the answer is "yes," then we should take their interests into account. Peter Singer (1946–) took this idea further, arguing that we should consider the interests of humans and animals equally.

Equal consideration
In Singer's view, animals try to avoid suffering, just as humans do—so we should consider their interests equally.

"In suffering, the animals are our equals."
Peter Singer

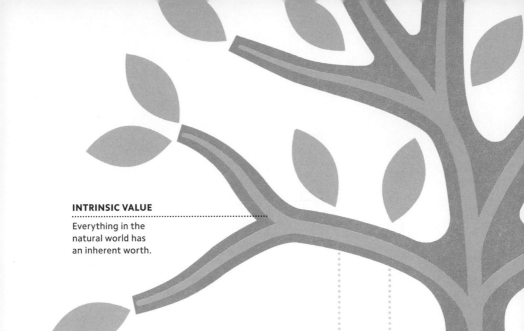

INTRINSIC VALUE
Everything in the natural world has an inherent worth.

DEEP ECOLOGY

Since humans settled into civilizations, they have tended to see themselves as separate from the natural world and to believe that it exists for their benefit—a resource for them to exploit. In the 20th century, the consequences of this attitude—such as climate change—prompted an environmentalist movement, which continues to grow. Philosophers such as Arne Naess (1912–2009) argued for what he called "deep ecology." Naess suggested that people should learn to see themselves as part of the natural world and value nature for its inherent worth rather than for what can be gained from it.

HUMAN GAIN
People may overlook nature's inherent worth, seeing it in terms of how it can benefit them.

POLI
AND P

T I C S
O W E R

Political philosophy is the study of the relationship between the individual and the state (the institutions of government). A key topic is whether the state is an artificial construct or a genuine expression of our social natures. Philosophers also question the nature of political power and study how governments justify their authority. Their concerns include whether citizens owe allegiance to their governments, the difference between democracy and tyranny, the balance between personal liberty and the common good, and the conditions under which governments can be legitimately overthrown.

> "There will be no end to the troubles of states ... until philosophers become kings."
> Plato

WISE LEADERS

Plato argued that political decisions should not be made directly by ordinary citizens, because they have an imperfect understanding of concepts such as justice and virtue. He claimed that philosophers, who have a better understanding of such concepts, are the best people to govern, because they are motivated by the truth and the interests of the city-state. Governments, he concluded, should be made up of a permanent, elite group of philosopher kings.

INCORRUPTIBLE

IMMUNE TO POOR ARGUMENTS

COMMITTED TO THE TRUTH

IN THE INTEREST OF THE STATE

IN THEIR OWN INTERESTS

Monarchy
The rule of one person for the benefit of the whole community.

Tyranny
The rule of one person for the benefit of that person alone.

Aristocracy
The rule of the wealthy and those who own property as a result of their virtue.

Oligarchy
The rule of a few, whose power comes from wealth rather than virtue.

Polity
The rule of the middle class for the benefit of the state as a whole.

Democracy
The rule of ordinary citizens in the interest of the poorer at the expense of the rich.

WAYS OF RULING

Aristotle identified three types of government: by the individual (monarchy), by the few (aristocracy), and by the many (polity). He argued that each can deviate into a degraded form if it fails to pursue the common good. For Aristotle, when governments pursue private interests, monarchy becomes tyranny, aristocracy becomes oligarchy (government for the rich), and polity becomes democracy.

CHOSEN BY HEAVEN

The Mandate of Heaven is the ancient Chinese political idea that an emperor gets their authority from heaven but can only keep it if they govern for the benefit of the people. A similar idea—known as the divine right of kings—became popular in 17th-century Europe, but with a key difference: European monarchs believed that they had authority from God to rule regardless of their behavior. The political theorist Robert Filmer (c.1588–1653) defended the divine right of kings in his book *Patriarcha*. He claimed that the true model of all government is that of the father, whose authority within the family is a God-given right.

"To majesty or sovereignty belongeth an absolute power."
Robert Filmer

Ruler
Legalist government is set up to preserve the absolute authority of the ruler.

Ministers
Officials carry out the ruler's wishes but are subjected to punishments if they fail.

People
The people are made to obey and are not trusted by the state.

STRICT CONTROL

Writing during the Warring States era, Chinese statesmen Shang Yang (390–338 BCE) and Han Fei Tzu (280–233 BCE), among others, argued for a state philosophy known as legalism, which required people to submit wholly to state rule. They considered people selfish and untrustworthy and advised that rulers govern them using strict laws and punishments. Ministers enacting the law would be rewarded or punished, depending on how well they performed their duties.

CHAOS IS WORSE THAN TYRANNY

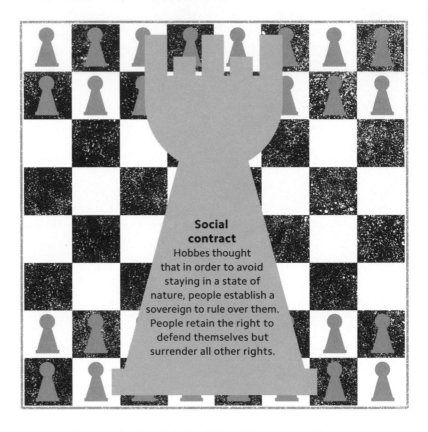

Social contract
Hobbes thought that in order to avoid staying in a state of nature, people establish a sovereign to rule over them. People retain the right to defend themselves but surrender all other rights.

Writing during the English Civil War, Thomas Hobbes argued that although kings do not have a divine right to rule (see p.122), sovereigns, or supreme rulers, are essential for maintaining order in society. He claimed that they gain their authority from their citizens, who, being competitive and aggressive by nature, depend on the ruler to protect them and maintain order. In a "state of nature" (without a government), life would be "nasty, brutish, and short," and people would willingly give up their freedom for the sake of being governed.

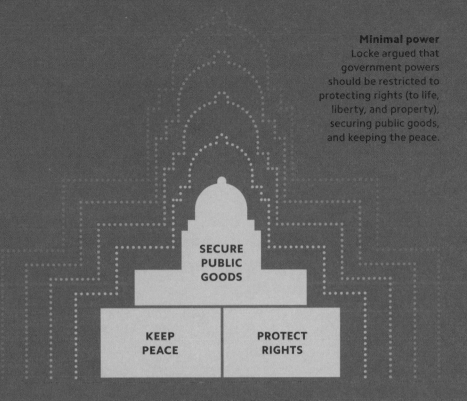

Minimal power
Locke argued that
government powers
should be restricted to
protecting rights (to life,
liberty, and property),
securing public goods,
and keeping the peace.

SECURE
PUBLIC
GOODS

KEEP
PEACE

PROTECT
RIGHTS

PROTECTING NATURAL RIGHTS

In the late 17th century, John Locke argued that government power should be limited. He believed that, in the state of nature (a period of time before governments were set up), people had natural rights, including the right to property, and that governments were established to safeguard those rights. Like Thomas Hobbes, he claimed that a government's authority rests on the consent of the citizens (see opposite). However, he argued that the people are also entitled to rebel if their government fails to protect their rights.

RULE BY THE PEOPLE

Jean-Jacques Rousseau (1712–1778) believed that people are cooperative by nature but that governments create inequality, which in turn leads to social unrest. He looked for a way in which people might enjoy the benefits of government without such problems. Rousseau's answer was popular sovereignty: a system in which decisions are made directly by citizens—for example, through referendums on particular issues—rather than by elected representatives. In such a system, people are in charge of their own political destiny, and decisions are expressions of what Rousseau called the "General Will."

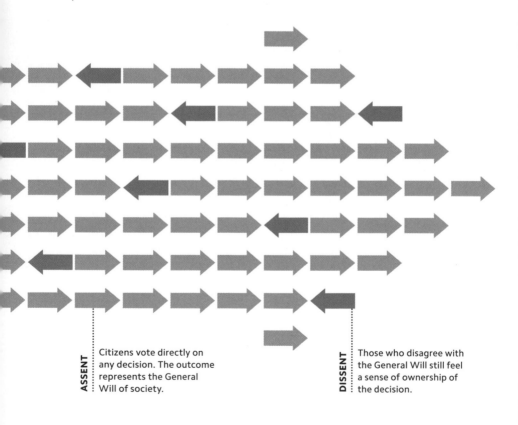

ASSENT Citizens vote directly on any decision. The outcome represents the General Will of society.

DISSENT Those who disagree with the General Will still feel a sense of ownership of the decision.

THE MARKET KNOWS BEST

SUPPLY

DEMAND

> "It is not from the benevolence of the butcher, the brewer, or the baker that we expect our dinner, but from their regard to their own interest."
> Adam Smith

In *The Wealth of Nations*, Adam Smith (1723–1790) argued that the government should not interfere with the economy. He claimed that the best way to create wealth is to leave the market to regulate itself—or, as he put it, to allow the "invisible hand" of the market to find a balance between supply and demand. However, Smith was not a libertarian (see p.137). He believed that the government has a vital role in providing the legal framework required for the market to work well.

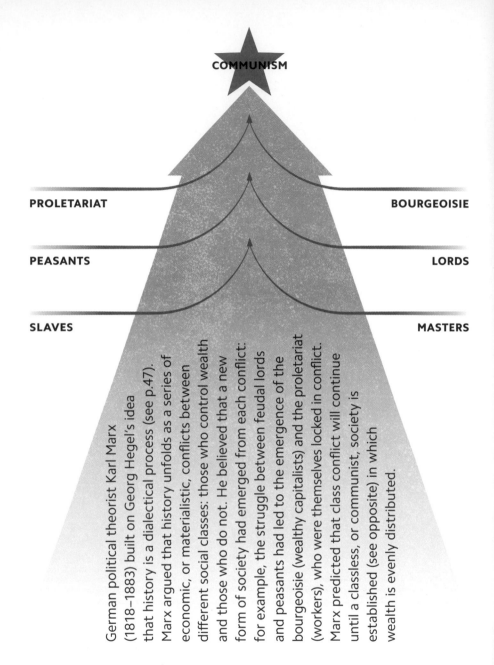

COMMUNISM

PROLETARIAT   BOURGEOISIE

PEASANTS   LORDS

SLAVES   MASTERS

German political theorist Karl Marx (1818–1883) built on Georg Hegel's idea that history is a dialectical process (see p.47). Marx argued that history unfolds as a series of economic, or materialistic, conflicts between different social classes: those who control wealth and those who do not. He believed that a new form of society had emerged from each conflict: for example, the struggle between feudal lords and peasants had led to the emergence of the bourgeoisie (wealthy capitalists) and the proletariat (workers), who were themselves locked in conflict. Marx predicted that class conflict will continue until a classless, or communist, society is established (see opposite) in which wealth is evenly distributed.

CLASS CONFLICT

A WORKERS' SOCIETY

Karl Marx envisaged communism as a new economic order in which social classes would vanish and the ownership of the means of production (for example, factories) would be shared by all—as would profits from labor. Marx thought that this new order would be established when working people's dissatisfaction with their capitalist, class-based society sparked a revolution (see opposite). The state, as an instrument of class rule, would then wither away and be replaced by elected boards representing the workers.

"From each according to his abilities; to each according to his needs."

Karl Marx

FALSE CONSCIOUSNESS

The term "critical theory" refers to a body of work developed by the Frankfurt-based Institute of Social Research. Its members—Max Horkheimer (1895–1973), Theodor Adorno (1903–1969), and others—tried to understand why German Marxism had failed to resist fascism in the 1930s, and to explain why a communist revolution had not occurred in Europe. They argued that in capitalist societies, revolution is obstructed when the media and advertising companies impose false needs on the public—such as the pursuit of ever more consumer goods. The Marxist term "false consciousness" refers to the state of mind created by these needs, which prevents people from resisting capitalism.

Blinded by capital
Critical theorists argued that capitalism blinds people to the fact that they are being exploited— which in turn stops them from showing dissent.

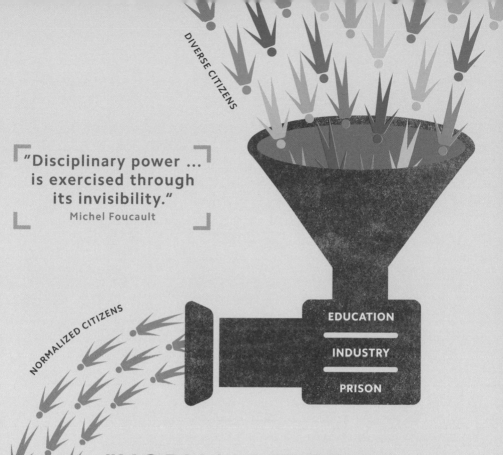

DIVERSE CITIZENS

NORMALIZED CITIZENS

EDUCATION

INDUSTRY

PRISON

"NORMAL" PEOPLE

Michel Foucault thought that not all power works through a figure of authority repressing the basic freedoms of others. He described a kind of power that relies on laws and systems of surveillance. No longer anonymous in a group or class, individuals know that they can be identified and punished if they break the rules, so they begin to conform. Disciplinary power operates in and through institutions to produce people who are "normal." According to Foucault, this power is most obvious in prisons, but it also operates in other social institutions, such as schools and workplaces.

CONTROLLED
BY THE STATE

After World War II, philosophers such
as Hannah Arendt (1906–1975) and Karl
Popper (see p.61) examined the concept
of "totalitarianism," which was used to define
both the fascist governments of Mussolini and
Hitler and the Stalinist regime of the Soviet
Union. They argued that both systems were
enemies of democracy and that both
promoted the view that societies could
be "perfected." Carl Friedrich (1901–1984)
and Zbigniew Brzezinski (1928–2017)
also claimed that the two systems
were similar: the governing party alone
could make decisions; no other political
parties were tolerated; a single leader
personified the government; and the
state controlled the economy.

Enforced ideology
A totalitarian government dominates
all areas of people's lives. It achieves
this through surveillance, control of the
media, and state-driven intimidation.
All citizens are expected to conform
to the state's view of society.

"One ever feels his two-ness— an American, a Negro; two warring souls ..."
W. E. B. Du Bois

PSYCHES OF THE OPPRESSED

W. E. B. Du Bois (1868–1963) coined the term "double consciousness" to describe the dual, conflicting identities experienced by people of color living in a racist culture. He used the phrase to define the experience of being both Black and American and the inner struggle faced by African Americans living in a society in which their predecessors were slaves. Frantz Fanon (1925–1961) later explored how Black people living in colonized countries experienced Blackness. He argued that white colonial cultures link "Blackness" with impurity, which causes colonized people to see their own skin color and culture negatively and to aspire to a white identity.

ABOLISH THE GOVERNMENT

In the 19th century, supporters of anarchism saw the state as an instrument of social control: a means by which one social class oppresses another. Anarchists base their opposition to government rule on the belief that people do not need to be coerced, taxed, or represented by a central political authority. They support the idea of a stateless society in which people organize themselves into local co-operatives, each promoting freedom, equality, and social harmony. French political activist and author Pierre-Joseph Proudhon (1809–1865) embraced this ideology and was the first self-declared anarchist.

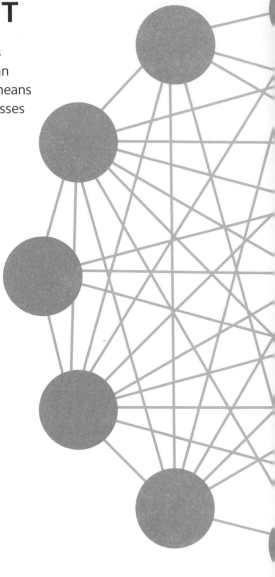

No state rule
Anarchists envisage an interconnected network of numerous, self-governing communities in which no one has authority over another.

JUSTIFYING THE STATE

STATE

From the early 20th century onward, statism (a political system in which centralized government has control over most social and economic affairs) was an increasingly widespread response to large-scale problems in Western societies. For example, in 1933, US president Franklin D. Roosevelt introduced the New Deal in response to the Great Depression. His massive program of state intervention sought to provide welfare, social security, economic support, electrification, and construction schemes across the country. As a result, the US federal government expanded its role and increased its influence over the nation's economy.

State control
In a statist system, communities are governed by a large, central state that aims to regulate economic and social affairs.

JUSTICE AS FAIRNESS

John Rawls (1921–2002) argued that a just society is one that rational people would agree is fair. He put forward the idea that if people were unaware of their gender, race, natural talents, or social status, they would not structure a society in which some groups or individuals were disadvantaged. Instead, he believed that people would support a redistribution of wealth—to provide a safety net for the vulnerable—and equal access to social institutions such as the education and healthcare systems.

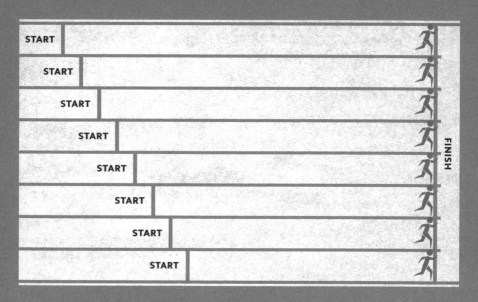

> "The principles of justice are chosen behind a veil of ignorance."
> John Rawls

Head start
Rawls argued that people are born unequal and that a fair society is one in which the greatest benefits are given to the least advantaged.

JUSTICE AS FREEDOM

Robert Nozick (1938–2002) disagreed with John Rawls's idea that a fair society is one in which wealth is redistributed (see opposite). He argued that if people were free to choose the kind of society that they would live in, they might choose one in which they are rewarded for taking risks—including the risk of being disadvantaged. Nozick claimed that wealth belongs to individuals and that the state should not interfere with the individual's right to succeed where others might fail. He supported libertarianism: the idea that the state should be limited to ensuring individual freedoms.

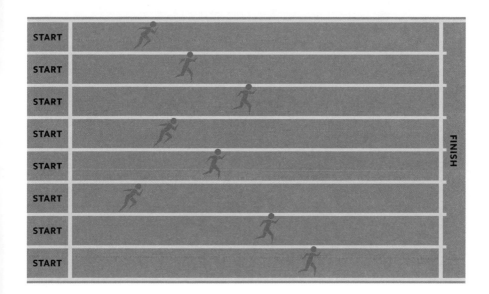

Free to win
Nozick thought that people have different talents and that they should be rewarded for using them, regardless of wealth distribution.

EQUALITY OF THE SEXES

Feminist political philosophers explore the gender inequality that exists in patriarchal (male-dominated) societies. Mary Wollstonecraft (1759–1797) challenged the traditional idea that women are by nature intellectually inferior to men. Instead, she claimed that society limits women and teaches them to be submissive to men. Later, Simone de Beauvoir (see p.68) argued that womanhood itself is a construct created by patriarchal societies, which define women as passive and maternal. Modern feminist philosophy explores how patriarchy ties into other forms of oppression faced by women: for example, by women of color, LGBTQ+ women, and disabled women. This idea of overlapping types of oppression is called "intersectionality," a term coined by Kimberlé Williams Crenshaw (1959–).

> "People are different from each other."
> Eve Kosofsky Sedgwick

Patriarchy

Most societies in history have been patriarchal (male-dominated) and oppressive toward women.

Feminism

Feminist philosophy supports feminist activism, which aims to free women from patriarchal oppression.

Equality

Feminists believe that the patriarchy must be dismantled in order to bring about equality for all sexes and genders.

INFINITE IDENTITIES

Queer theory expands on earlier gay and lesbian studies to look more broadly at gender, sexuality, identity, and power. Early pioneers—including Judith Butler (see p.69), Michel Foucault (see p.70), and Eve Kosofsky Sedgwick (1950–2009)—shook up conventional thinking about sex, gender, and desire by claiming that people's identities are shaped by ideas rather than by biology. One of the key concepts of queer theory is heteronormativity: how society reinforces the idea that heterosexuality is "natural" and therefore "normal." Today, queer theory is a broad field of study including many different aspects of gender and sexuality, but it still seeks to challenge heteronormative ideas.

LOGI
ARGU

C AND
M ENT

Logic explores the reasons why some arguments are better than others. A logical argument consists of a conclusion supported by a set of statements called premises. To analyze an argument, we examine whether the premises are true and whether the conclusion follows from them. Aristotle produced a system for recognizing logical arguments, and philosophers used it for two millennia—until Gottlob Frege invented a new system of formal logic in the 19th century. Logic also includes the study of fallacies (bad arguments), so that we can detect them in both our own and other people's thinking.

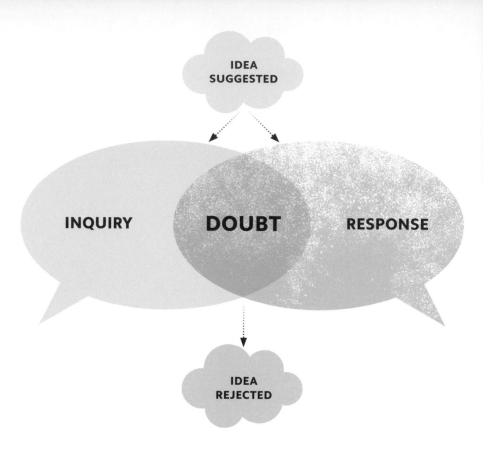

QUESTIONING ANSWERS

According to Plato, Socrates (c.470–399 BCE) engaged in a type of argument known as *elenchus*. First, he identified a claim that his opponent believed to be true (which was usually about the nature of something, such as courage). Then, by asking questions, he got his opponent to agree with further claims about the subject. Finally, he showed that these further claims were inconsistent with the original claim, demonstrating that his opponent should not have believed it in the first place.

THE SYLLOGISM

First described by Aristotle, the syllogism is a form of deductive argument (see p.144). It has three sentences: a major premise, a minor premise, and a conclusion. Together, these sentences have the logical form of: all Xs are Ys, Z is an X, therefore Z is a Y. According to this logic, agreeing with the premises makes it impossible to deny the conclusion, which means that the argument is valid. Each sentence has a subject (for example, "cats") and a predicate (a quality of the subject: for example, "animals") and a verb that connects them (for example, "are").

A TIGER IS AN ANIMAL

A TIGER IS A CAT

ALL CATS ARE ANIMALS

CONCLUSION
The conclusion tells us that a "tiger" is an "animal."

MINOR PREMISE
The minor premise contains the word "cat" and tells us that a type of cat is a "tiger" (the subject of the conclusion).

MAJOR PREMISE
The major premise contains the word "cats" (which is in both premises) and the word "animals" (the predicate of the conclusion).

> "Knowledge must rest on necessary basic truths."
> Aristotle

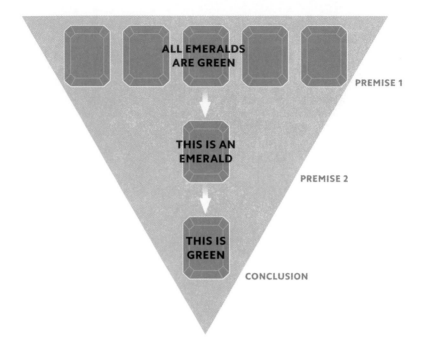

ALL EMERALDS ARE GREEN — PREMISE 1

THIS IS AN EMERALD — PREMISE 2

THIS IS GREEN — CONCLUSION

A LOGICAL CONCLUSION

A deductive argument is one in which the conclusion must be true if the premises are true—purely as a matter of logic. A good deductive argument is known as valid. If it is also sound (its premises are true), then its conclusion is certain. On the other hand, a bad, or invalid, deductive argument is one in which the conclusion could be false, even if the premises are true. If there is no logically possible situation in which the premises of an argument are true and its conclusion is false, then the argument is valid.

A PROBABLE CONCLUSION

Unlike a deductive argument (see opposite), an inductive argument is one that does not provide certainty but makes a given claim more or less probable. The words "valid" and "invalid" are therefore not used for inductive arguments. A good, or strong, inductive argument is one in which the conclusion is highly probable if the premises are true. The probability of the conclusion of a bad, or weak, inductive argument is raised very slightly if the premises are true. Further evidence can make a strong inductive argument weak or a weak inductive argument strong.

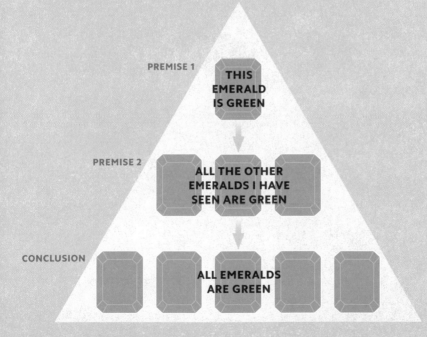

PREMISE 1

THIS EMERALD IS GREEN

PREMISE 2

ALL THE OTHER EMERALDS I HAVE SEEN ARE GREEN

CONCLUSION

ALL EMERALDS ARE GREEN

EVALUATING ARGUMENTS

Assessing arguments involves answering two questions: "Does the conclusion follow from the premises?" and "Are all the premises true?" If the answer to the first question is "yes," then the logic of the argument is good. This gives us conditional knowledge: if the premises are true, then the conclusion is either true (in the case of a deduction, see p.144) or probably true (in the case of an induction, see p.145). If the answer to the second question is also "yes," then the argument is sound: its conclusion follows from its premises, and its premises are true.

Good argument

The conclusion of a good argument always follows from its premises. However, if any of the premises are false, then the conclusion might also be false. Good deductive arguments are described as "valid." Good inductive arguments are described as "strong."

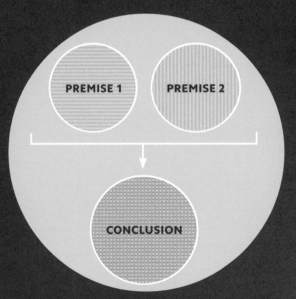

PREMISE 1   PREMISE 2

CONCLUSION

Sound argument

If an argument is sound, then its conclusion follows from its premises, and its premises are all true. This means that the conclusion of a sound deductive argument is true and the conclusion of a sound inductive argument is probably true.

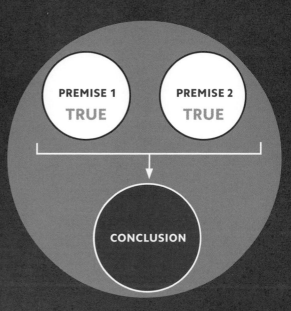

PREMISE 1
TRUE

PREMISE 2
TRUE

CONCLUSION

SOUND ARGUMENT

GOOD ARGUMENT

Logic and truth

Every sound argument is good, but not every good argument is sound. A good argument is unsound if any of its premises are false, though it is still good in a logical sense (that is, its conclusion follows from its premises).

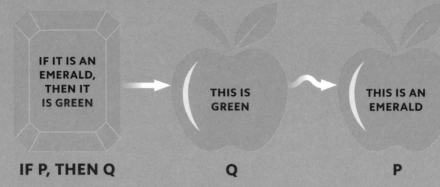

IF IT IS AN EMERALD, THEN IT IS GREEN

THIS IS GREEN

THIS IS AN EMERALD

IF P, THEN Q **Q** **P**

Bad structure
Formal fallacies depend on an argument's structure. The example shown above resembles the valid argument "If P then Q, P, therefore Q," but it is incorrectly structured as "If P then Q, Q, therefore P." This is known as "affirming the consequent."

SPOTTING BAD ARGUMENTS

Fallacies are bad arguments that are frequently mistaken for good arguments. People often reason badly, but such reasoning is only fallacious if it resembles good reasoning. False beliefs can arise from bad arguments, but they are not in themselves fallacies. Likewise, sarcasm and exaggeration can win arguments, but they are not necessarily fallacious. Fallacies are patterns of faulty reasoning that, because they are so frequently mistaken for patterns of good reasoning, have been studied and categorized. Learning about fallacies is useful because it helps us spot them in our own and other people's reasoning.

> "Begging the question is proving what is not self-evident by means of itself."
> Aristotle

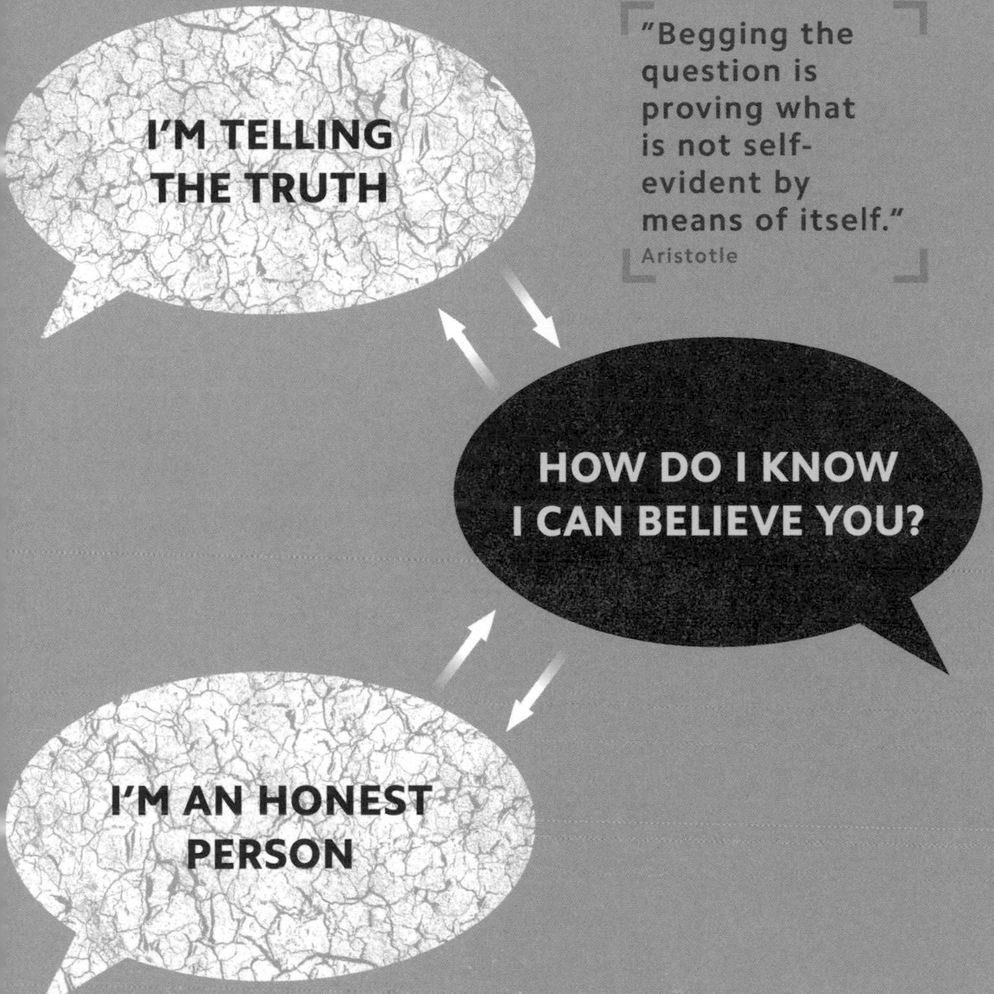

I'M TELLING THE TRUTH
HOW DO I KNOW I CAN BELIEVE YOU?
I'M AN HONEST PERSON

Bad content
Informal fallacies depend on the content of an argument rather than on its structure. In the example shown above, the argument is only valid because it is circular—that is, its conclusion is contained in its premises. This is known as "begging the question."

HYPOTHESIS

EXAMINING EVIDENCE

When observing a phenomenon, a scientist may notice a pattern. The scientist may then propose a hypothesis—a general rule derived from their observations. In order to test the validity of such a hypothesis, scientists carry out experiments. If the results of these experiments do not prove that the hypothesis is false (see p.61), then it can be accepted as a scientific theory. However, that is not to say that it is necessarily true; further experiments or observations may disprove it or show it to be only partially true.

OBSERVATION

EXPERIMENTATION

THE LOGIC OF SIMPLICITY

Sometimes several theories are put forward to explain a phenomenon, and we have to decide which is most likely to be correct. William of Ockham (c.1280–c.1349) suggested that the best way to choose between theories is to start with the simplest. Known as "Ockham's razor" (because it cuts out complexity), the rule that Ockham used states that a good theory contains just enough ideas to explain a phenomenon and should be chosen over one that involves unnecessary assumptions or complexity. The same principle applies to arguments: a strong argument is one that relies on the fewest assumptions, because any one assumption may turn out to be wrong.

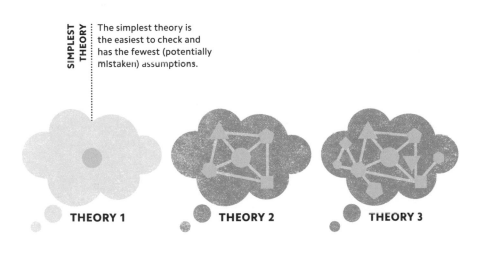

SIMPLEST THEORY

The simplest theory is the easiest to check and has the fewest (potentially mistaken) assumptions.

THEORY 1　　THEORY 2　　THEORY 3

"It is useless to do with more
what can be done with less."
William of Ockham

PREMISE ONE

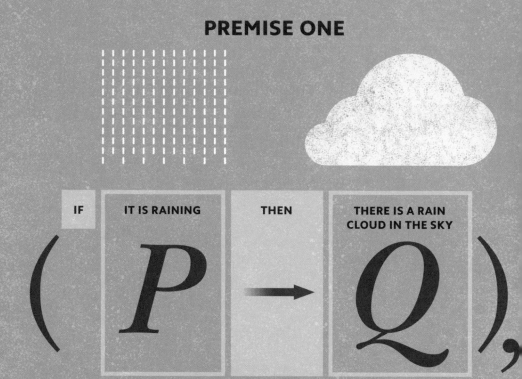

IF	IT IS RAINING	THEN	THERE IS A RAIN CLOUD IN THE SKY
(	*P*	→	*Q*),

LOGICAL STRUCTURES

Propositional calculus focuses on the structure rather than the content of arguments. To use it, the first step is to identify which sentences of an argument are its premises and which is its conclusion. Then letters (for example, P, Q) are used to stand for the sentences and symbols to stand for the logical words that connect them (for example, → for "if … then …"). Round brackets indicate the letters to which the symbols relate, and the turnstile symbol (⊨) stands for "therefore." The turnstile indicates that the conclusion (to its right) follows logically from the premises (to its left).

PREMISE TWO

CONCLUSION

IT IS RAINING	THEREFORE	THERE IS A RAIN CLOUD IN THE SKY
P	⊨	*Q*

Propositional formula
The letters and symbols in this propositional formula show the structure of the argument, "If it is raining, then there is a rain cloud in the sky. It is raining, therefore there is a rain cloud in the sky."

"The structure of the sentence serves as a picture of the structure of the thought."
Gottlob Frege

LEAVES

GREEN THINGS

UNIVERSAL QUANTIFIER

$$\forall x$$

UNIVERSAL QUANTIFIER

The universal quantifier, ∀, stands for "all," as in "All leaves are green" (which is formally written as "Everything, x, is such that if x is a leaf, then x is green").

EXISTENTIAL QUANTIFIER

The existential quantifier, ∃, stands for "at least one," as in "At least one leaf is green" (which is formally written as "There is at least one thing, x, such that x is a leaf and x is green").

EXISTENTIAL QUANTIFIER

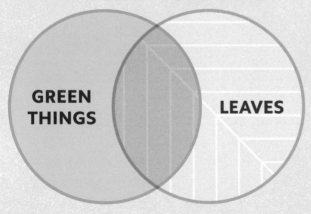

GREEN THINGS

LEAVES

$$\exists x$$

**THERE IS AT LEAST ONE
THING, X, SUCH THAT**

| IF | X IS A LEAF | THEN | X IS GREEN |

$$(\ Lx \rightarrow Gx \ )$$

USING QUANTIFIERS

Predicate calculus builds on propositional calculus (see pp.152–153) by introducing symbols for terms such as "all" (∀) and "at least one" (∃). Predicates (see p.143) are incomplete concepts; for example, the phrase "is green" refers to a class of green things but says nothing about its members. Predicates can be completed with designators, such as in "That leaf is green"; with universal quantifiers, such as in "All leaves are green"; and with existential quantifiers, such as in "At least one leaf is green."

$$(\ Lx \ \& \ Gx \ )$$

| X IS A LEAF | AND | X IS GREEN |

INDEX

Page numbers in **bold** refer to main entries.

ACKNOWLEDGMENTS

DK would like to thank the following for their help with this book: Phil Gamble and Mark Cavanagh for the illustrations; Alexandra Beeden for proofreading; Helen Peters for indexing; Senior Jacket Designer Suhita Dharamjit; Senior DTP Designer Harish Aggarwal; Jackets Editorial Coordinator Priyanka Sharma; Managing Jackets Editor Saloni Singh.

The publisher would like to thank the following for their kind permission to reproduce their photographs:

23 Dreamstime.com: Vladimir Il'yin / Wladbvbh.
154 Dorling Kindersley: John Devolle.

All other images © Dorling Kindersley
For further information see:
www.dkimages.com